Virginia Woolf & Vaness

Remembering St Ives

Marion Dell and Marion Whybrow

Virginia and Vanessa playing cricket in the garden at Talland House

First Published in paperback 2004

Tabb House
7 Church Street,
Padstow, Cornwall, PL28 8BG

ISBN 1-873951-46-9

Cover, from the painting *Skidden Hill*, St Ives, 1910, by Claude Francis Barry.

Book design by Kim and Joseph Lynch, Lelant, Cornwall.

Printed by Marksprint, Brighton, Sussex

Working in St Ives harbour, c.1900

Contents

St Ives Town

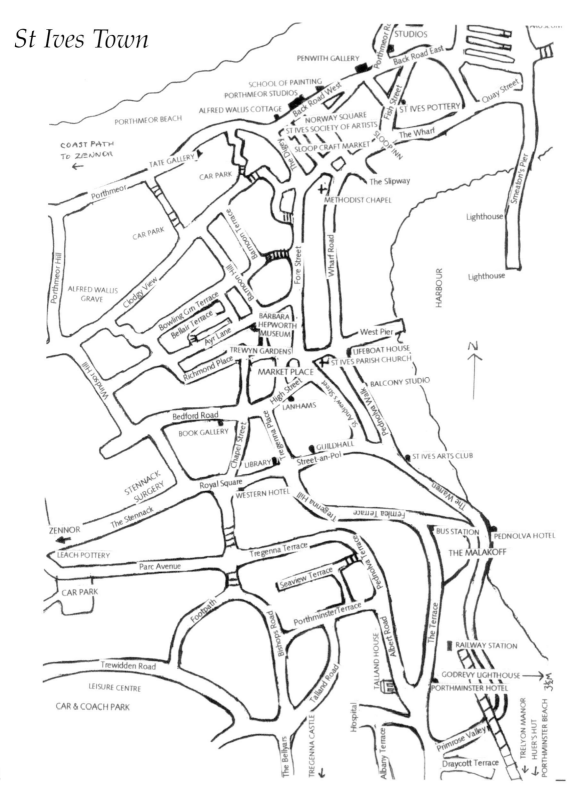

St Ives: *a town on 'the very toe-nail of England'*

The town was then much as it must have been in the sixteenth century, unknown, unvisited, a scramble of granite houses crusting the slope in the hollow under the Island. It must have been built for shelter; for a few fishermen, when Cornwall was more remote from England than Spain or Africa is now. It was a steep little town. Many houses had a flight of steps, with a railing leading to the door. The walls were thick blocks of granite built to stand the sea storms. They were splashed with a wash the colour of Cornish cream; and their roughness was like the clot of cream. There was nothing mellow about them; no red brick; no soft thatch. The eighteenth century had left no mark upon St Ives, as it has so definitely upon every southern village. It might have been built yesterday; or in the time of the Conqueror. It had no architecture; no arrangement. The market place was a jagged cobbled open place; the Church was on one side; built of granite, ageless, like the houses; the fish market stood beside it. There was no grass in front of it. It stood flush to the market place. There were no carved doors, large windows, no lintels; no moss; no comely professional houses. It was a windy, noisy, fishy, vociferous, narrow-streeted town; the colour of a mussel or a limpet; like a bunch of rough shell fish clustered on a grey wall together.

Virginia Woolf [1]

Introduction

Childhood is a repository of images on which the human being will draw for the rest of his or her life. Marion Dell and Marion Whybrow tell the story of two Victorian sisters in a house by the sea, who will grow up to be Virginia Woolf and Vanessa Bell. This book looks back beyond the formidable artists in words and paint that the sisters became, to the children they were.

Marion Whybrow and Marion Dell bring two very different voices and complementary areas of expertise to their exploration of the potent role which St Ives played in the lives and creative work of Virginia Woolf and Vanessa Bell. Marion Whybrow's extensive knowledge of St Ives as an art colony has already led her to write the definitive book on the subject. She places in context the early artistic development of Vanessa Stephen, and traces the influences she encountered among the painters who flocked to St Ives in the late nineteenth century. Marion Dell combines deep knowledge of Virginia Woolf's writing with a zestful, atmospheric approach to her early life and family history. She argues that the roots of Woolf's writing lie as much in place as in experience, and that her passionate, sensuous response to place is at the heart of her fiction.

We go back to a house above Porthminster Beach, Talland House with its two or three acres of garden, where the Stephen family spent their long summers. Here in St Ives, the young Virginia and Vanessa learned to play cricket, swim, boat, tramp across country, hunt moths, fish rockpools, and explore the unique character of the little town on the edge of the Atlantic.

It's important to emphasise that these were not summer holidays in the sense that we understand them nowadays. As Marion Dell explains, it was the removal of an entire household, with servants and 'mounds of luggage'. The family arrived in St Ives for a few months each summer. During those formative years, Vanessa and Virginia Stephen had two homes and two lives, and it's arguable that their St Ives life left the deeper impression.

Marion Dell offers clear and moving evidence that St Ives was always Woolf's land of lost content. Without those early years by the sea, and the images which they laid down in her brain and senses, Woolf would have been a different writer, and perhaps a lesser one. It is hard to imagine Virginia Woolf without the St Ives childhood memories which shaped *To the Lighthouse, The Waves,* and to a certain extent *Jacob's Room.*

The influence on Vanessa Bell is more difficult to gauge. She left less direct evidence in her painting than Woolf did in her writing. But Marion Whybrow offers compelling support for the idea that the artistic life of St Ives was a powerful influence in the development of Vanessa Bell as a painter. Vanessa Bell would have seen artists painting and sketching en plein air on the beaches, in the lanes, or on Smeaton's Pier. Newlyn and St Ives were not artistic backwaters. Artists who worked here were in the forefront of new approaches to painting, and they knew it. Through family friendships, Vanessa got to know artists such as Walter Sickert. She visited studios and attended exhibitions. She was beginning her own long apprenticeship in drawing and painting, and at the same time she was learning how a wide range of professional artists worked and how they lived. Importantly, Vanessa might also have observed that there were women, such as Elizabeth Stanhope Forbes, among the painters whose work was exhibited and admired.

So we go back to the nursery, looking out over the bay to Godrevy. The house boils with children and visitors. It resounds to the demands of their needy, overwhelmingly emotional father, Leslie Stephen. But within this chaos and play and work and purposes, two female children think about what they would like to do with their lives. They discover that each has a vocation: one to write, the other to paint. They talk about this remarkable fact, and make plans. There will be huge obstacles and many delays, but what is striking is that these two Victorian girls should conceive such ambitions at all. Their family was by no means one which encouraged women to enter professions. They were intended to be beautiful, charitable, charming, intelligent, devoted, the promoters of male achievement rather than the realisers of their own dreams.

It may be, as both authors of this book suggest, that the sheer physical freedom of their St Ives life helped these sisters to conceive of independent achievement. Their winter life, in London, was constricted by decorum and chaperonage. London girls of the upper middle-class in the late nineteenth century did not run or roam. They walked in certain ways, took their exercise in certain parks, and dressed in accordance with strict codes. But in St Ives there was the large garden with its path running down to the beach, the wide beaches themselves, day-long rambles in the wild countryside of West Penwith, and explorations of the intricate, salty little fishing town. Both girls must have developed greater hardiness and self-confidence. Even within the house, there was no need to be tidy or to take care of the furniture. It was all old stuff, ramshackle. If a chair stood on its four legs, that was good enough. Doors were flung open to the sun and the salt breeze.

The opposed values of London and St Ives foreshadowed the battle which these girls would later fight and win. They would abandon the conventional life of the upper-middle class girl going into society before a suitable marriage. They would shock their friends and family by going off to live in Bloomsbury in a style considered reprehensibly bohemian, and they would achieve their goals of working as writer and artist.

From childhood, neither Virginia nor Vanessa Stephen saw themselves as amateurs. They knew they had an enormous amount to learn, and they aimed to achieve a professional level in their work. They read, studied, took lessons, made copies, observed the work of others, questioned, discussed. They confided in each other and supported each other. Marion Dell quotes from *To The Lighthouse*, where the children, 'as stealthily as stags' disappear from the dining-table to their bedrooms, where they can talk about their inner lives, of which their parents know little. Talland House in the 1880s and early 1890s was a place of secrets. Its haunting emotional quality, as much as the loveliness of its setting, possessed both Virginia Woolf and Vanessa Bell throughout their lives. There is a letter in which Bell describes the overwhelming emotion with which she first read *To the Lighthouse*. She recognised that her sister, like the fictional painter Lily Briscoe in the novel, had struggled to create a work of art which revealed inner truth as well as outer appearance. And she had done so. Woolf, like Lily Briscoe, 'had had her vision'.

Marion Dell and Marion Whybrow reveal how powerfully the 'vision' of both Woolf and Bell sprang from their early life in St Ives. When they were thirteen and fifteen, they lost both their mother and their home in Talland House. Their childhood could not be revisited, and for both of them the transition to adulthood was hard. They had to fight convention, family pressures, their own inward misery and their bereavement. Cut off by time and death, St Ives might have become merely a source of regrets, unhappy longing and nostalgia. But Virginia Woolf and Vanessa Bell were tougher than that. They held on to the childhood images within them, in all their clarity, just as they held on to their ambitions. Vanessa Bell had learned what it was to be a painter, to work in the open air, setting down the freshness and immediacy of image, to visit studios facing into pure north light and learn from the painters there, to draw and draw and draw until her eye was in, to be ruthless in what she discarded. Virginia Woolf, similarly, would draft and redraft for decades until she could transform the images within her - garden, lighthouse, mother wrapping a shawl around a skull to shield a child from nightmare, tapping of blind-cord, tumult of emotion and desire - into the greatest of art.

*St Ives and the
Land's End peninsula*

❦ *Prologue - St Ives*

Nothing that we had as children was quite so important to us as our summer in Cornwall.

Virginia Woolf [2]

St Ives, when discovered by Leslie Stephen on a walking tour of Cornwall, was a 'fish odiferous' town. Its population relied on the fishing industry. Its harbour, in the days of pilchard fishing and processing, was the hub of activity, with its seine boats, fish auctions, packing factories, and horses and carts to transport salted and pressed barrels of pilchards from the harbour. There were boat builders along the sandy foreshore, where new boats were launched into the sea, direct from the workshop. Cornish luggers and seine boats for catching pilchards filled the bowl of the harbour, dwarfing the tiny cottages

Leslie Stephen, Julia, Stella, Adrian, Thoby, Vanessa and Virginia

with their huge canvas sails. Men, women and children were involved in the work, which supported their daily lives.

Leslie Stephen bought the lease of a house in this working town in 1881. The following year, Leslie, a sophisticated man of letters, of some wealth and literary renown in the metropolis of London, brought his young family to live for a few months each year in this very different, rather primitive environment. The Stephen family were Leslie and his wife Julia, with the children from her first marriage:

George, Stella and Gerald Duckworth; and Laura, Leslie's daughter from his first marriage: and Julia and Leslie's children: Vanessa, Thoby, Virginia and Adrian (born 1893). Vanessa would grow up to become the noted artist Vanessa Bell, and Virginia the famous writer Virginia Woolf.

St Ives is a small town built on sand at the edge of two seas, between the safe haven of the harbour and the threatening Atlantic ocean with its huge surfing seas, sweeping the rocky coast on the twenty mile journey to Land's End.

Smeaton's pier, built in 1770, protecting the harbour, has an attractive round stone-built lighthouse with a viewing gallery around the top. The building of an extension to the pier, with its second octagonal iron-clad lighthouse, was completed in 1890. The Stephen family, who stayed in the town over a period of thirteen years, must have witnessed the building of this additional lighthouse and quay on their annual holidays

Cottages in Back Road East, c.1900

in St Ives. West Pier was added in 1894 and used for off-loading stone from local quarries.

The cottages are made of local building materials, Cornish Delabole slate and granite. Narrow cobblestone lanes separate the houses, fish cellars, and net lofts. The Stephens' home was an elegant building with spacious grounds above the town. Talland House, with its balconied windows, overlooks the great expanse of water of St Ives Bay, out to Godrevy lighthouse and beyond. The four younger members of the family would spend up to three months in their ideal home, accompanied by Mr and Mrs Stephen and Stella who, in August 1893 at the age of twenty-four, wrote in her diary: 'Ginia Thoby & Adrian went off to fish (caught nothing!) Father botanised. Mother went round of Roaches Crays etc. Nessa & I sat in garden, she painted I worked – cricket with Dick as usual.' This particular holiday ended on October 9th when Stella recorded the family's departure. 'Left St Ives. A large party. Lisa Georgie 3 ch[ildren]. & 4 servants. 2 compartments in corridor train. Train 1 hour late. Gerald met us'[3]

The Branch Line

For some years the Great Western Railway had served Cornwall from Paddington to Penzance, the end of the line to the West country. However, in 1877 with the building of a branch line, the steam locomotive the Cornish Riviera arrived at St Ives station. This produced a significant increase in the tourist trade. The station was built above Porthminster beach and the seine boats now sheltered beneath a railway bridge. In due course the boats disappeared and Victorian bathing tents gave way to wind breaks, surfboards, and the present-day holiday-maker. Passengers change at St Erth for the local train to St Ives. It travels four and a half miles along the picturesque coastline, starting with Lelant and the waterbird sanctuary, opening out at the Hayle estuary to a view of Godrevy lighthouse and the bay; it crosses the golf course on the sand dunes above the vast area of Porthkidney beach, into

Carbis Bay, through the wooded area, until it rounds the bend and catches the breathtaking view of St Ives harbour. People alight almost onto the fine sun-bleached sands of Porthminster beach, where the clear blue sea gently laps the shore.

St Ives Station in its heyday

Fishing

When Leslie and Julia Stephen brought their family to St Ives, the fishing industry was still the major source of employment. Leslie, although not interested himself in catching fish, had great sympathy for the fishermen and their hazardous trade. To support the fishing industry there were a number of coopers making barrels, or hogsheads, for packing pilchards for export to Italy, sailmakers to provide the brown sails typical of St Ives luggers, ropewalks for weaving ropes, net-making factories, salt cellars, and smoke houses for curing fish. There were many family-owned boats and most cottages had their own cellar for storage of fishing gear or for pressing fish to extract the oil and brine, with a flight of stone steps leading to the living quarters.

There were seasons for catching mackerel, herring and pilchards. In the summer crab pots were placed in the sheltered bays off St Ives to

Packing pilchards in barrels

catch shellfish. There was also long-lining for hake, dogfish, plaice, whiting and ray. But it was the pilchard for which St Ives was best known. They came into the bay in their millions from late summer to December. Seine boats were lined up ready at Porthminster beach awaiting the cry of 'Hevva', blasted through loud hailers, from the watchful huers on a high vantage point overlooking the bay. The Stephens' friend, Edward Hain, interpreted the antics of the wildly gesticulating huers, explaining how they were directing boats towards the shoals of fish by signalling in a kind of semaphore with furze bushes. The seine boats would put out and trap the pilchards in a circle of nets where they were held in a heaving mass of silver until the small boats, known as dippers, scooped up the fish and ferried them to shore. The pilchard was largely exported to Mediterranean countries:

Huer signalling position of pilchard shoal

A feature of Porthminster beach in my youth was the fleet of big, tarry seine boats drawn up on the fore-shore and up the valley - three hundred of them, each with attendant tow-boats and bearing its owner's mark brightly coloured upon its black bows. [4]

Mining

Although fishing was the major occupation of St Ives, tin and copper mining played an active role in the area surrounding the town, and in neighbouring parishes. When the fish were in short supply mining helped provide a temporary income. Mines opened and closed in quick succession. As well as deep mining, open cast mining was carried out on hillsides above the town. Rosewall Hill, which towers over St Ives, is full of holes in the ground and the remains of abandoned workings. All over Cornwall the ruins of engine houses rear up out of the landscape and perch on the edges of cliffs, where mine workings were tunnelled under the sea.

The Decline of Fishing and Mining

This lively and necessary life-maintaining fishing industry gradually declined, and by 1900 St Ives had lost much of its fleet; pilchards were either over-fished or the shoals gathered elsewhere. Fishermen joined

Seine netting for pilchards

other fishing fleets around the coast of Britain.

The fleet for large-scale fishing in Cornwall is centred in Newlyn. Today, the few fishing-boats left in St Ives harbour are largely engaged in fishing for mackerel, or ferrying holidaymakers to Seal Island, but always on standby are the inshore and deep-water lifeboats of the Royal National Lifeboat Institution.

Tin mining was also in decline. Miners lived in nearby Halsetown, a new model village, built by a benevolent mine owner James Halse, to house miners in sturdy buildings with their own gardens, or they lived in terraced houses along the Stennack stream, which flowed down the valley to St Ives to discharge into the sea. Stennack means place of tin. Many miners emigrated to South Africa, Australia and America where their skills were needed, rather than starve in Cornwall. Such was the rate of emigration that it is said that in every hole in the ground in any country, there are Cornishmen, using their inherited mining skills in the new world.

St Ives harbour, 2003

Farming

Like all rural communities, there was a great reliance on farming, which supported the fishermen and miners' families, and all folk were engaged in harvesting. Farming, mining and fishing lived side by side all the way from St Ives out towards the area known as West Penwith and on to Land's End. Edward Hain, of the Hain Shipping Line, owned much farming and mining land and from 1900 to 1912 he built grand houses, in the style of manor houses, for his tenant farmers, believing they should live in comfortable dwellings. These can be seen dotted about the landscape on the way to Zennor. Close to town there were small field systems on the cliffs at Man's Head worked by St Ives folk. Some grew daffodils for market and others food for the family. The remains of these field patterns, with their stone hedges, can still be seen on the cliffs. People living in St Ives also owned their own pig. These were largely held at Porthgwidden and slaughtered in the town. Porthgwidden is now a beautiful sandy cove favoured by families with small children.

Shipping

Treloyhan Manor, home of the Hain family

It is amazing that so small a town as St Ives could be the birthplace of a major shipping company. It began with the Hain family, resident in the town since the sixteenth century. Edward Hain founded the company in 1816, having a part share in a sailing lugger *Dasher*, which was built and registered in St Ives. There were four generations of Edward Hain, who not only managed the business but were also master mariners. The fourth Edward showed no interest in going to sea but expanded the business and purchased steamships.

This new fleet he named after Cornish

place names, all beginning with Tre- as in Trevalgan, the name of a hill and farm near St Ives. Trevalgan means the place of a mighty prince. It is therefore apt that the great St Ives artist and Cornishman, Peter Lanyon, who died as the result of a gliding accident in 1964, has a plaque to his memory on a huge boulder on Trevalgan Hill. Tre- can mean dwelling place, farm, homestead or village and in the Hain fleet there were fifty-six vessels with the Tre- prefix. The company had offices in London and St Ives and the fleet traded from major ports in the UK. When visiting the London office, Mrs Hain took the opportunity to pay her respects to the Stephen family at Hyde Park Gate.

The success of the Edward Hain shipping company can be seen in the large house Mr Hain built in extensive grounds above St Ives town in the 1890s. In 1893 Stella Duckworth recorded in her diary: 'Mother Nessa

Miss Hain, Lady Hain & friend on the Wharf

and I went to Hain[s] Palace. Met Mrs H coming here but went to see the Palace with her. Nice house not beautiful 14 bedrooms . . . rather large for the 2 little Hains and their 3 ch[ildren].'[5] Treloyhan Manor is now a Christian holiday centre.

Edward Hain was a stalwart of the town, serving on the Town Council and elected for six terms of office as Mayor. He was elected MP for St Ives from 1900-'06. In 1912 he was knighted for his services to British shipping. However, Sir Edward was denied the possibility of passing on the shipping business to the fifth Edward, his son, when the young man was killed at Gallipoli in 1915, while serving as a captain with the Cornish Squadron of the Devon Yeomanry. Two years later Sir Edward Hain died at Treloyhan Manor. The business was eventually sold to the P & O Shipping Company. Many fishing families in St Ives and neighbouring villages benefited from the sale of small shares, and it is well remembered when a local fishing-boat sailed into the bay for the signing of contracts with the P and O.

St Ives and the Artists

Today, St Ives is largely unchanged. It is one of those magical places that people visit and return to again and again. Artists and writers have been attracted to this beautiful town for over a century, where a large art colony has been established. They are pulled by a thread that lures creative people to its indefinable magnetic quality, and allows their artistic genes to flourish. They paint in pure light mirrored by fine white sands and unhindered by pollution. It is a charming place, renowned for its five sea-washed sandy bays, its harbour, and its ability to sustain credibility in various descriptions of loveliness.

The Arrival of the Artists

The first artist of note to arrive was J.M.W. Turner in 1811, who made several sketches of the town. Before the turn of the nineteenth century a large colony of artists had established itself. They were drawn by the remote area, the quality of light, the untouched rural community, the marine environment, and all the romantic ideas of artists who had travelled on the Continent to France and Brittany and found there ideal places to live and paint. Maria and Harewood Robinson were among the early arrivals in St Ives in 1884. Most of the painters had visited the artists' colonies of Pont Aven and Concarneau in Brittany, and the two

Artists & onlookers c.1900

Cornish harbours of St Ives and Newlyn, just ten miles apart, reflected these ideals and offered the same facilities.

The artist Harewood Robinson noted that 'Old sail lofts and cottages were sought out, and turned into studios, and large skylights appeared everywhere among the grey roofs of the old town; by the enterprise of the townspeople new studios were built, some of imposing size, and St Ives took its place as a world-known centre of art work.' [6]

Catch of Pilchards
1895, Fred Sargent

Porthmeor Studios in Downlong

It is true to say that the arrival of artists in the town of St Ives re-floated the economy. As fishing declined the artists flourished, and the local

population was ready to adapt to a new lifestyle. Artists began occupying large premises, which had usually housed fishing gear, and the renamed Porthmeor studios were described in the *Western Echo* newspaper in 1902 as 'very commodious, with good approach and all of them with a northern aspect and splendid sea view.' It is thought they were built as sail lofts around 1850, as part of a group of lofts extending the length of Porthmeor beach. The huge upper

Porthmeor Studios

floors were converted to studios, while the lower part still housed the fishermen's boats, tackle and fish nets. This is still true today.

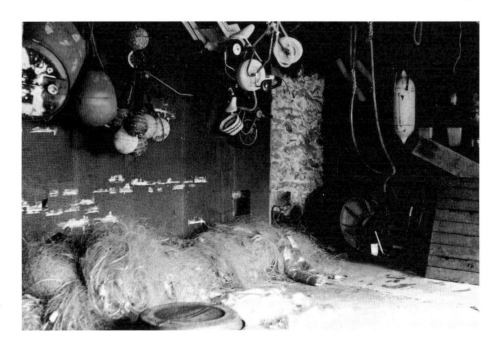

Fishing gear under Porthmeor Studios

Fishermen and artists reside together with neither encroaching on the others' territory, and respect is accorded to both occupations. These are the only surviving studios and sail lofts still in existence on Porthmeor beach; they face the Atlantic, and back onto the old fishing quarter of the town, where cottages huddle against wind and tide.

The First Artists' Club

To provide for their needs, the artists set up their own societies as places to discuss and exhibit their work. The first of these was St Ives Arts Club, founded in 1890 by the artist Louis Grier, who described its location: 'we are in view of the glorious bay and in sound of the cry of the hovering gull, and under our feet comes the roar of the ground-sea as it struggles with the rocks at the base and rushes madly up the granite walls of our foundation. It is a very marine spot indeed.' [7]

In 1908 Charles Marriott was president of St Ives Arts Club and, as such, he wrote an article for the *Daily Mail* on the present state of the artists' colony: 'At the present moment, of the eighty odd studios in this little town of St Ives there is not a single one to let. Cornwall is becoming more and more emphatically the centre of English art, and this winter marks the highest point the development has yet reached.'

Charles Marriott lived at 3 Porthminster Terrace in St Ives for seven years, with his wife and two daughters. It was there his son was born and where he wrote his first successful novel *The House on the Sands*. He left to become art critic for *The Times*, and so became acquainted with the work of the Bloomsbury painters.

In 1927 St Ives Society of Artists was formed and established an art gallery. In 1949 a breakaway group formed the Penwith Society of Arts. These latter two house the different styles of painting; the first shows mainly traditional land/seascapes, and the second the more modern and abstract works. These two artists' institutions, together with the Arts Club, are still functioning.

Several schools of painting have flourished in the area, run by practising artists. The first was established in 1895 by Julius Olsson and Louis Grier. Their School of Landscape and Marine Painting offered 'an opportunity of studying out of door effects.' Most advertisements for schools stressed the importance of painting *en plein air* in the European tradition, with such artists as Algernon and Gertrude Talmage, and Charles and Ruth Simpson.

The St Ives School of Painting, founded in 1938 by a husband and wife, Leonard Fuller and Margery Mostyn, continues to provide facilities for visitors and local artists at all levels of development. Practising artists resident in the town teach the students. St Ives can claim to be one of the largest art colonies with an unbroken record from the 1880s to the present day. Pupils can call on the local expertise in portraiture, life classes and the environment. The school is now managed by a Trust.

Artists and Methodists

The general consensus of the townsfolk on that first influx of artists was 'Well, if they can work in the same conditions as us, they can't be too bad.' However, the living conditions of the native Cornish were harsh, with large families to raise, no indoor sanitation and typhoid still a major child killer. There was always the threat of the workhouse and the asylum, and sickness and starvation were a constant spectre. However, the strict Methodist teaching prevalent at the time probably helped the women cope with their poverty and loss of children. To die was to go to heaven, a far brighter place than they ever would experience on earth.

W.H.Y. Titcomb

The artist William Holt Yates Titcomb, friendly with a local Cornish family, visited their cottage to say goodbye before travelling to Italy to paint. On coming into the room he saw the grandmother propped up in bed, the light of ecstasy on her face. She was going to her maker, he was told. Two fishermen sons came to offer prayers, while the daughter wept at her side. Back from Italy a year later, the artist returned to the cottage

Piloting her home,
W.H.Y. Titcomb

and found the old lady alive and well. Titcomb had never forgotten the scene he first witnessed and persuaded the family to pose, recreating that event in his studio. The painting, *Piloting Her Home*, was shown at the Royal Academy in 1894.

Three large drawings of Titcomb's, which he developed into paintings, hang on the walls of the Primitive Methodist Chapel in Fore Street. Titcomb presented the drawings to the chapel in 1924. Accompanying the drawings is a letter from a woman in Australia in which she states that the strength of the picture *Piloting Her Home*, seen in an exhibition, was the sole reason for her converting to Methodism.

The Sloop Inn

The fishermen of St Ives used to meet the artists of the town in the Sloop Inn, just off the harbour slipway. Town records show that the inn has been in existence for 400 years. Some of the rafters are ships' timbers. It has been painted and photographed thousands of times. It is said that every artist who visited the town has turned up at the Sloop. One could visit the inn to find local people and painters standing alongside their portraits or caricatures. Art exhibitions have been hosted there for a century and still take place. What have disappeared are the fishing-boats from the harbour, and the fishermen.

The Sloop Inn, c.1900

Upalong

Many artists built grand houses above the town, overlooking the bay. This is known as Upalong, where the gentry lived. These houses had gardens and could house family and servants comfortably, while also providing studio accommodation:

It was possible to get an excellent servant for as little as £10 a year. She had one evening a week free and a few hours to herself on Sunday; and although this seems almost like slavery, for the most part they felt themselves one with the family; on good terms with their master and mistress and often adored the family.[8]

There was a good supply of servants in the town who could live out and provide every requirement of a household, as well as the local tradespeople, who brought provisions and services daily. Although the Stephen family brought their own servants to Talland House, they still employed local gardeners and a housekeeper to maintain the premises in their absence. With such a large household, local provisions were in great demand.

A large employer of staff for both house and garden was Edward Hain at Treloyhan Manor. Harewood Robinson and his wife Maria were both artists, and close neighbours of the Stephen family. Their house Belyars Croft, with studio attached, is now a hotel. In 1910 the seascape painter Julius Olsson built his house St Ia, now a hotel, on the main road leading into St Ives. His studio adjoins the house. Olsson's other studio was at Porthmeor. Moffat Lindner acquired Chy-an-Porth, on The Terrace, and added considerably to this already substantial house. He also owned Porthmeor Studios, which he rented out to artists, and occupied one himself. Studio No.5 housed in succession the artists Borlase Smart, Julius Olsson, Ben Nicholson and Patrick Heron.

A Change of Scene

From a population almost totally dependent on one industry: fishing, the townsfolk were happy to rent out rooms and houses to visiting artists and students, who opened up spaces to light and colour. Their easels appeared on every cobbled street, and from the countries of America, Finland, France, Germany, Sweden, Australia and New Zealand, and all corners of the British Isles, the artists came flocking:

Epidaurous, Barbara Hepworth sculpture from The Malakoff

The fish-odoriferous town of St Ives is a veritable gem of beauty and inexhaustible in its attractions to artists. Whistler, struck with its charms, is said to have sketched it, and certainly many have done it since. Now there are some 200 studios tucked away in many an odd corner of the place, forming a little colony of the artistic world. [9]

The incoming artists, all of independent means, employed the local population as housekeepers, maids, nannies, gardeners and cooks. They spent money freely in the town. In the fishing port of Newlyn the same transformation was taking place. It continues to the present day, with new studios being built or converted from the ruins of sail lofts. Artists still find St Ives a congenial place to live, work, and show their paintings in the many art galleries. Gallery owners from across the country come to trawl for pictures painted in St Ives.

Tate St Ives

The building of Tate St Ives, which opened in 1993, is another remarkable achievement for so small a town. The art community was largely responsible for raising the money by the auction of a great sale of their paintings: 250 works of art were donated. The auctioneer, David Lay, and his staff gave their services free, and together with a variety of other events, raised £150,000. This great effort was successful in attracting other monies.

In the 1940s St Ives art colony underwent a sea change, with the arrival of artists with radical ideas and a progressive approach to modern art. They invested their paintings and sculpture with a feeling for place, a spirituality, an understanding of the power that Cornwall exerts on creative people. It is because of their contribution to abstract art that St Ives continues to be acknowledged as a world-renowned centre for the development of modern art.

The Tate Gallery discovered in its London collection a great number of works from such sculptors as Barbara Hepworth and Naum Gabo, and the painters Ben Nicholson, Patrick Heron, Terry Frost, Bryan Wynter, Peter Lanyon, Karl Weschke, Wilhelmina Barns-Graham, and many others who came to St Ives from the 1940s onwards and changed the face of modern art. They added a new dimension to purely visual representations of beautiful scenery. This collection is now housed in its own gallery, Tate St Ives. It stands on the edge of the wild Atlantic Ocean overlooking the beautiful, unspoilt, Porthmeor beach. It is the final accolade to a town that has created and housed over a century of art and artists.

Tate Gallery, St Ives

Patrick Heron

Patrick Heron spent much of his childhood in St Ives. His father Tom was a partner and director in the unique textile company of *Crysede*, with the designer Alec Walker. They produced fashionable garments in silk and crêpe-de-chine from factories based in Newlyn. The St Ives branch was established in 1926. In London during this time Vanessa and Duncan were involved in designing fabrics for Allan Walton's textile company. Vanessa produced designs in large repeat patterns. Other artists involved in designing for the two companies were C.R.W. Nevinson, Frank Dobson (with whom Vanessa exhibited in 1941) and Cedric Morris. The latter artists had also lived and painted in Cornwall.

In 1947 Patrick Heron rented a cottage in Downlong. His balcony studio overlooked the harbour and the two piers. From the windows he painted a series of pictures of objects and figures in the room and the scene without, of boats and the harbour, split up by the intersection of the window frames.

In 1955 Patrick bought Eagle's Nest, the house he had visited as a child and coveted since. Virginia and Leonard Woolf had stayed there with friends many times. The house sits astride a rocky hillside, taking the full force of winds blowing in from the Atlantic. It overlooks farmland, with fields which drop to the sea, and the hamlet of cottages that were once the homes of D.H. Lawrence and prominent painters such as Wilhelmina Barns-Graham and Karl Weschke. The village of Zennor is several fields distant, famous for its attraction to writers and painters. Eric Quayle, writer and bibliophile, housed his 16,000 books in a house leading down to Zennor Cove.

At Eagle's Nest Patrick and his wife Delia further developed the gardens begun by Will Arnold-Forster:

Ladder at Eagle's Nest

As the garden was on top of a hill topped by a rocky outcrop, there were large slabs of granite and big boulders everywhere. The real forte of this garden were the camellias, rhododendrons and azaleas . . . Pink, purple and white heaths of all sizes . . . grew round the rocks. Brilliant flame trees, Embothrium, flowered in the cave garden below a rocky precipice, to which one descended by a long flight of stone steps or climbed precariously down by a wooden ladder. [10]

Patrick Heron lived and painted at Eagle's Nest, and in his Porthmeor studio. His garden had a direct effect upon a series of particular paintings, but it wasn't until he saw his house and land from the air, that he realized that these paintings with their stripes and daubs of colour were his garden paintings. He had to accept that those colours, shapes and forms had moved him and etched themselves into his subconscious.

Patrick died in 1999 and is buried in Zennor. His contribution to the St Ives Tate Gallery is the large stained glass window in the entrance foyer. It is the largest single sheet of glass in the world, with no connecting lead strips to hold pieces together. This would have spoilt the overall design, which is about large areas of colour. The whole design is laminated between sheets of glass for strength.

Barbara Hepworth

The sculptor Barbara Hepworth arrived in 1939, with her triplets and painter husband Ben Nicholson, to escape the bombing in London. Ben left St Ives in 1958. That same year Barbara received a CBE. She said 'I owe St Ives a tremendous debt: living here has meant a very great deal to my work. It is not just landscape, but the community, the town and everything about the place.'[11] She was resident in St Ives until her death in her Trewyn

Patrick Heron at Eagle's Nest

Studio in 1975. Her sculpture can be found in many public places in the town, as well as in her studio and garden, managed by the Tate Gallery. In the Lady Chapel of St Ives Parish Church is one of her finest pieces, a sculpture of *Mother and Child*, carved by Dame Barbara in memory of her son from her first marriage, Paul Skeaping, who died in an air accident over Thailand in 1953.

Dame Barbara Hepworth is a sculptor who made St Ives uniquely her own. Her work, as with so many other sculptors, painters, writers and creative people is a reflection of her love for this exceptional town. Clearly, we see a similar effect on the powerfully evocative writing of Virginia Woolf. In the childhood memories and love of St Ives for Virginia, and her artist sister Vanessa, lay the foundations for their chosen careers.

Barbara Hepworth garden

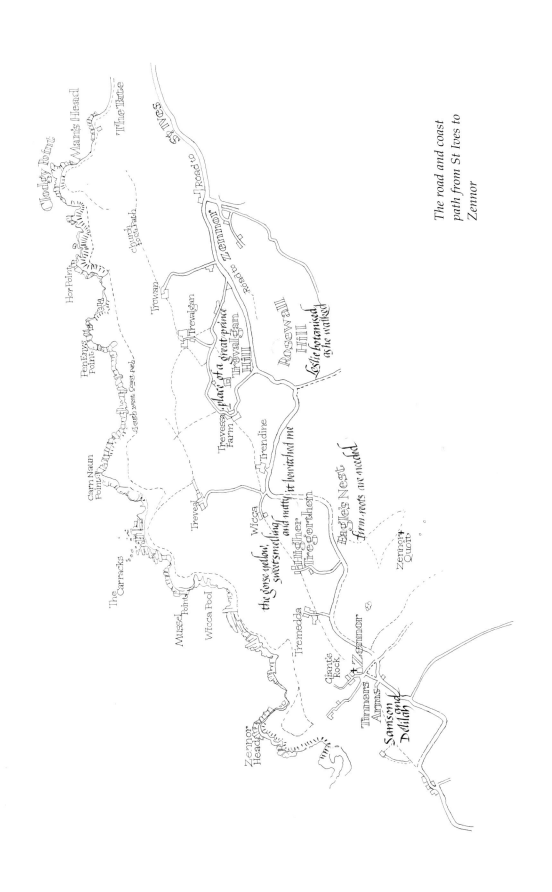

The road and coast path from St Ives to Zennor

Clodgy Point
Man's Head
The Tribe
St Ives
Road to
Zennor
Road to Zennor
Hor Point
Church footpath
Trowan
Trevalgan
Trevalgan Hill
Trevessa Farm
Rosewall Hill
Leslie botanised as he walked
Pen Enys Point
South west Coast Path
part of a great prince
Trendine
the gorse yellow, sweet-smelling
Eagle's Nest
and nutty; it bewitched me
from roots are needed
Carn Naun Point
Treveal
Wicca
Hellsner
Tregerthen
Zennor Quoit
The Carracks
Mussel Point
Wicca Pool
Tremedda
Giant's Rock
Zennor
Zennor Head
Timmer's Arms
Samson and Delilah

Talland House in the 1880s: 'a square house, like a child's drawing of a house; remarkable only for its flat roof, and the crisscrossed railing that ran round the roof '.

Talland House 2002

Talland House

When they took Talland House father and mother gave us –
me at any rate – what has been perennial, invaluable.

Virginia Woolf[1]

Talland House is an elegant villa on the outskirts of St Ives in Cornwall. It was the Stephen family's holiday home from 1881 until 1895. In 1882, the first summer they went there as a family, Vanessa was three years old and Virginia only a few months.

For the sisters, Virginia and Vanessa, their time living at Talland House and exploring St Ives and the countryside around it was a life-long source of personal pleasure, shared memories, and creative inspiration. Virginia fictionalised the house, her parents and their summers in St Ives in her famous novel *To the Lighthouse*, published by the Hogarth Press in 1927, for which Vanessa illustrated the dust jacket.

The dust jacket for To the Lighthouse designed by Vanessa Bell

Talland House was never a grand house; its appeal lay in its location and in the free and relaxed way of life which they were able to pursue there. The lightness and space contrasted strongly with the confined darkness of their London house and the foggy gloom of London winters. It became a haunted, and a haunting, house embodying the ghosts of their childhood, which they were to remember for ever.

Leasing Talland House

Talland House had been newly restored after a fire in December 1873, allegedly caused when the son of the house accidentally knocked over a lamp. When Leslie Stephen bought the lease it was an uncharacteristically spontaneous and liberal gesture and one which had very happy conse-quences. Virginia was to reflect with surprise that such was the

ease and amplitude of those days that a man to whom money was an obsession
thought it feasible to take a house on the very toenail, as he called it, of England.[2]

The expansion of the railway was making St Ives accessible to an ever-increasing stream of artists, walkers and tourists who could get there from London easily in a day. Virginia and Vanessa remembered the long journeys on the Cornish Express from Paddington and the increasing excitement as they arrived at St Erth where they transferred to the branch line for the brief final leg of their journey. With servants and mounds of luggage they finally arrived in St Ives at about 7.00 in the evening. Talland House was then part of the Tregenna Castle Estate, which had been bought by the Great Western Railway Company. Many of the Stephens' friends, especially Henry James, the American novelist, who wanted more comfort, space and quiet than was available at Talland House, often stayed at the nearby, luxurious, Tregenna Castle Hotel.

Tregenna Castle
Hotel in the 1880s

From a look-out point in their garden the Stephen family could watch for the signal to indicate trains arriving and set off for the station just below their house. There they met a stream of family members and friends who visited them each summer. One such arrival is recorded by the ten year old Virginia in her family newspaper, the *Hyde Park Gate News,* in suitably high flown journalese language and with endearing inaccuracies:

Mr Fisher arrived at the ancient borough of St Ives on Saturday afternoon. The felicious family of Stephen were posed on a convenient bank awaiting the arrival of the locomotive. In due time it came. Paterfamilias, Materfamilias and family rushed down to meet their renowned relation. Oh 't was a happy sight to see! We leave the rest to the imagination's vivid course as we are sure dear reader that you possess that faculty in it's highest degree.[3]

Herbert Fisher, Julia's brother in law, was Vice-Warden of the Stannaries, the court that regulated the tin mining industry. His position, unfortunately, was less exacting than it had been because of the decline of the Cornish tin trade. It was only necessary for him to come to Truro about four times a year but he would stay whenever possible with the Stephens at Talland House. His son, also called Herbert, had very happy memories of playing with his cousins there.

Family Life

It was a small house for a large family. Talland House was worn and faded but always welcoming. Virginia's fictionalised description of the house rings true. Mrs Ramsay

saw the room, saw the chairs, thought them fearfully shabby. Their entrails . . . were all over the floor; but then what was the point, she asked herself, of buying good chairs to let them spoil up here all through the winter when the house, with only one old woman to see to it, positively dripped with wet? . . . and there was room for visitors. Mats, camp beds, crazy ghosts of chairs and tables whose

London life of service was done – they did well enough here; and a photograph or two, and books. . . . If they could be taught to wipe their feet and not bring the beach in with them . . . things got shabbier and got shabbier summer after summer.[4]

Downstairs there was a large drawing room and a large dining room, with French windows opening onto the garden. This view found its way into *Jacob's Room*, where Jacob was invited to a dinner party. Behind the other guests he could see

Julia Stephen, Virginia, Vanessa, Thoby and Shag the dog, by the drawing room windows. Talland House, 1894

the grey-green garden, and among the pear-shaped leaves of the escallonia fishing-boats seemed caught and suspended. A sailing ship slowly drew past the women's backs. Two or three figures crossed the terrace hastily in the dusk. The door opened and shut. Nothing settled or stayed unbroken. Like oars rowing now this side, now that, were the sentences that came now here, now there, from either side of the table.[5]

Also on the ground floor was the 'back den' or smoking room, to which Leslie Stephen frequently escaped when bored by visitors. Then there was the bustling kitchen, which played a large part in the children's memories. It was just below the room that at one time was their night nursery, where they would let down a basket on a string from their window to the open kitchen window. If the cook, Sophie Farrell, was in a good mood the basket contained favourite titbits when it was drawn back up again; if not, it was empty or even cut off the string. They got to know local tradespeople and overheard gossip and St Ives' stories. Virginia remembered Mrs Adams who brought live blue lobsters and put them on the kitchen table and Alice Curnow who hauled huge baskets of laundry to and from the house. Upstairs were several smaller bedrooms and the two main front bedrooms with their beautiful wrought iron balconies. Here Virginia remembered her mother in a white dressing-gown surrounded by the passion flowers that grew up the front of the house.

One of the front rooms was always their parents' but other bedrooms were used differently as the children grew older and depending on who was staying at the time. Up some twisty wooden stairs were the attic bedrooms, which were also shared by the servants where thin partitions allowed sounds to be heard by all. Virginia vividly remembered hearing Stella Duckworth crying on the night she had refused Jack Hills' offer of marriage and a young Swiss maid grieving for her father. The sun pouring into the attics lit up

bats, flannels, straw hats, ink-pots, paint-pots, beetles, and the skulls of small birds, while it drew from the long frilled strips of seaweed pinned to the wall a smell of salt and weeds, which was in the towels too, gritty with sand from bathing.[6]

Julia Stephen and her daughter Stella Duckworth on the terrace at Talland House, 1894

St Ives seen from Stella Duckworth's bedroom window, 1890s

Postman

Sandrey Signalman.

Pascoe boatman

Mr John Roach, fisherman of HPG News. Sept 1892 Photographed by Gerald D. (double image)

A page from Virginia's photograph album showing the postman at the front door of Talland House, William Sandrey the signalman, and Pascoe the boatman, also at the front door. This photograph was taken by Gerald Duckworth experimenting with a double image, full face and profile, c.1892

A page from Virginia Woolf's photograph album showing A.L. Davies, Sophie Farrell the cook, Paddy the gardener, and Ellen Eldridge, c.1892

Another small staircase led from the attic outside to a flat area of roof fenced in by a balustrade. From here there were magnificent panoramic views and it was a specially good vantage point for watching the firework displays. Both Virginia and Vanessa, and later Vanessa's children and grandchildren, adored firework displays which still feature at Charleston celebrations.

While the house was full of people it was probably less cramped, and certainly much lighter, than 22 Hyde Park Gate, their home in London. To future artists it provided rich material. Much of it, including the sense of overcrowding, finds its way into *To the Lighthouse*, where

disappearing as stealthily as stags from the dinner-table directly the meal was over, the eight sons and daughters of Mr. and Mrs. Ramsay sought their bedrooms, their fastnesses in a house where there was no other privacy to debate anything, everything . . .[7]

Life there was not all holiday. The children continued their lessons in the dining room, often taught by Julia and sometimes by Leslie or one of the governesses who were periodically hired.

Julia giving her children their lessons in the drawing room at Talland House, c.1894

They were often French or German speaking but there is little evidence that they taught the Stephen children much in those languages, and, if Virginia's newspaper accounts are to believed, were sometimes more interested in reading French novels on the beach than looking after their young charges. Julia continued her philanthropic works visiting the poor and sick. Leslie continued his writing, especially on the *Dictionary of National Biography,* working such long hours that his health often suffered.

Visitors

Although the Stephens only came as a family in the summers Leslie Stephen often came alone at other times, especially when the children were very young, and they sometimes let friends use the house out of season. It was, moreover, always filled with friends. Visitors were listed in the Weekly Summary and Visitors' List in the local newspaper. On August 24th, 1889, for instance, Mr and Mrs Leslie Stephen and family have listed staying with them at Talland House: Mr John W. Hills, Corby Castle, Carlisle; Dr Wolstenholme, Coopers Hill; and Mr W.C. Headlam, King's College, Cambridge. In the list published on August 31st, Mr Hills has left, Mr Wolstenholme and Mr Headlam are still there, and Mr H. Fisher and Mr W. Fisher have joined them. The list remains the same the following week. In the September 14th list, however, the guests are Mr F.W. Gibbs, Miss Lushington and Mr A.L. Davies, who are also listed as staying for two weeks. These friends were expected to take part in games, especially cricket, theatricals and expeditions to nearby beauty spots. Stella's friend Margaret Lushington often stayed with her at Talland House. She loved music, playing the piano and singing. The two indulged in 'girl talk' and confidences late into the night. Margaret's diary gives accounts of mornings spent writing letters, shopping expeditions into St Ives, blackberrying, walks to Knill's Monument or onto the beach, and the inevitable cricket. Stella's love of photography comes over clearly in her own diary entries and is often mentioned in Virginia's newspaper, especially when there were mishaps with broken or forgotten plates, or problems with the developing. Gerald also was a keen photographer. Family, guests and servants were asked to pose, sometimes reluctantly, for the camera. Happily for us, many of these photographs survive.

Margaret Lushington's Diary, 1893

Wednesday, September 13
Lovely morning quite hot I put on a white gown - Stella & I did a lot of songs & things & then we wrote & she & I & Mr Headlam went down to the Town. After lunch & letters we all toured down again & went & sat on the island & ate sweets - home to tea & cricket & then we all went down to meet Gerald who arrived very cheerful. Dinner & I played [the piano] til quite late ... bed 1.30.

Friday, September 15
Lovely morning we all went down to the Town & shopped extensively and I got all my letters done before luncheon, then we had grand cricket matches all the afternoon & I got a good bit of quilt done - conversation rather flaggy at dinner. After dinner I played [the piano] for hours & then Stella & I talked late. Bed 2.15.

Tuesday, September 19
Rain all night & in the morning so pleased that Mr Stephen who was all right again this morning - Poor little 'Ginia tho' was not well. In the morning we taught Mr Headlam Tonic Sol Fah & Mr Hocken the post-man poet arrived with his little girl - so nice, but mighty difficult to talk to! - ... We played cricket & games all afternoon & crowds of locals came to tea and then tip and run after tea ...

Thursday, September 21
Wet day again - in the morning Mr Norton read Matthew Arnold & Browning - out - so beautifully I worked & paid bills & then photographed & after lunch & letters we all went down to the town to see Mr Stephen give the Humane Society's medal - tea after at Dr Nichols ...

Stella Duckworth's Diary September 1893

27 Wednesday
Lovely warm day. Wore my blue crepe. Photographed Dick N & got him grapes for the journey...After lunch the boys & children started off on Hare & Hounds. I developed & toned. Children all back to Tea rather exhausted but nevertheless had cricket after tea. Tho's [Thoby's] last day; delightful walk on sands before dinner with Georgie.

28 Thursday
Pouring wet day. All saw poor old Tho. off. [Thoby was returning to boarding school at Clifton.] Mother Nessa going to St Erth with him. He seems to me much less happy at going back than usual perhaps because of cricket & everything is in full swing here with Georgie & Gerald. Whole family very low for the rest of the day. The boys & I rushed to the island before dinner & got very hot.

Margaret Lushington's and Stella Duckworth's diaries, 1893

The Garden

Leslie Stephen was particularly attracted to the garden when he first saw Talland House. There were a wooden gate and footpath up to the house and a garden covering two or three acres up a hillside. There was a stream, which flowed down through the garden, disappearing underground in places and appearing again to splash among rock pools. There were interesting hedged spaces and nooks and crannies, which more than compensated for the lack of space inside the house. Each area had

Virginia and Adrian playing cricket in the garden at Talland House, c.1892

its own family name and history. There was the Coffee Garden, and the Cricket Ground where they often played late into the evening with a ball painted with luminous paint. Both Vanessa and Virginia were renowned for their skill as bowlers and batsmen, Thoby even claiming that they were better than boys at his school. Young friends such as Hilary Hunt, Holman Hunt's son, and Dick and Rupert Brooke loved to play.

George, Gerald and Stella's future husband Jack Hills, all played and their friends such as Madge Symonds, the inspiration for Sally Seton in *Mrs Dalloway,* were pressed into joining in. There was an orchard, kitchen garden, strawberry beds, and huge glasshouses where grapes were grown, Julia's particular pride. Departing friends would often be given bunches of grapes to take back to London.

Julia also loved all the flowerbeds, and used to enjoy sitting in her sheltered Loo Corner and talking to friends under the trees. She spent much time matchmaking here. One of her successes, the match between

Leo Maxse and Kitty Lushington, was finalised in the Love Corner in 1890, overheard by the hidden Stephen children. Family photos and accounts record the many social gatherings here each summer, and give a picture of a noisy, boisterous, happy, extended family. Their young cousin William Fisher used to love sailing home-made paddle steamers, propelled by an elastic band, on the pond.

Talland House; looking across the tennis lawn to the glasshouses, c.1892

Family members such as Julia's mother Mrs Jackson, the Lushingtons, Stillmans and Symondses all stayed or visited regularly. James Lowell,

Stella with her brother George Duckworth on the left and her future husband Jack Hills on the right, in the glasshouses at Talland House, August 1892

the American Ambassador and Virginia's godfather, was a frequent visitor as was Henry James.

Their neighbour George Meredith read his poetry here to Julia. Mr Wolstenholme, a mathematician friend of Leslie Stephen transposed into Mr Carmichael in *To the Lighthouse*, dozed for hours in his wicker beehive chair.

Another of the main attractions of the garden was its views across the bay. The children often stood on one of the vantage points watching the many different boats and, of course, seeing Godrevy Lighthouse.

From the Lookout place one had then, a perfectly open view across the Bay. . . . It was a large Bay, many curved, edged with a slip of sand, with green sand hills behind; and the curves flowed in and out of the two black rocks at one end of which stood the black and white tower of the Lighthouse; and at the other end, Hayle river made a blue vein across the sand, and stakes, on which always a gull sat, marked the channel into Hayle Harbour. This great flowing basin of water was always changing colour; it was deep blue; emerald green; purple and then stormy grey and white crested. There was a great coming and going of ships across the bay. Most usually, it was a Haines steamer, with a red or white band round the funnel, going to Cardiff for coal. In rough weather, sometimes one would wake to find the whole bay full of ships, that had come in overnight for shelter . . . Then every morning the clumsy luggers went out, deep sea fishing; and in the evening there was the mackerel fleet, its lights dancing up and down; and the fleet

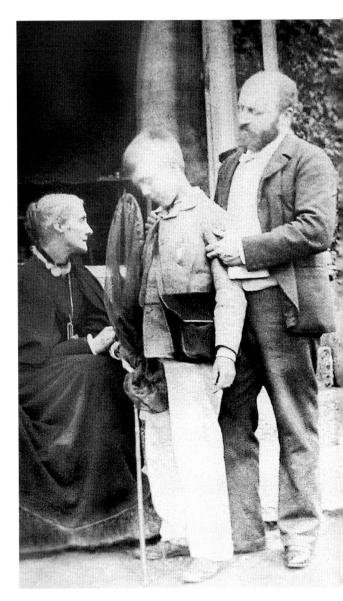

Julia, Henry James and Adrian with his fishing net, on the terrace at Talland House, c.1894

returning, rounding the headland and suddenly dropping their sails. We would stand with mother on the Lookout place watching them. [8]

The St Ives fishing fleet leaving Hayle, c.1890

The Beach

From the house a path led down through Primrose Valley, an area of gardens and orchards, to Porthminster Beach. Virginia always remembered looking down on the gardens so that the tops of the trees, laden with their red and golden apples, were at her eye level. These apples were a source of great pride to their owners, one of whom was Mr Lobb who came up to help in the garden at Talland House. The yield from Mr Lobb's young apple trees in Primrose Valley merited articles in the local newspaper in October 1892 and again in September 1893.

Often Julia took the younger children down to the Beach to paddle or poke around in the rock pools. There were bathing huts and safe places for swimming. Sometimes all the family went and Helena Swanwick, the artist Walter Sickert's sister, remembered seeing them playing there. When the Stephen family first went there the beach was relatively deserted but each year more and more tourists came, as was recorded in the local newspaper:

With the advent of our summer visitors, the beautiful Bay of St Ives is every day studded with many rowing and sailing boats, and our beaches present quite an animated appearance. Here may be seen 'young men' and maidens, old men and children, thoroughly enjoying the sands and health giving breezes: and Mr Pascoe, who is ever ready and willing to oblige his customers and to do every-thing for their comfort, is in attendance with the bathing tents, which are being well patronized. There is a great demand for apartments for August – indeed the applications are so numerous that it is impossible to accommodate all who would like to spend a few weeks in the quaint old town of St Ives.[9]

Virginia recorded in her own newspaper of August 8th the following year that, sadly, Mr Pascoe had renounced his position as bathing master.

Porthminster Beach, c.1904

The Area Around

The older children enjoyed swimming and picnics on the beach but they would also frequently go walking with Leslie Stephen, almost always accompanied by Shag their beloved dog, to collect moths or botanical specimens. Virginia's newspaper for July 18th, 1892 records Leslie's delight at finding a new plant specimen and his encouragement to his children to learn the 'difficult tribes' of plants. One of the great attractions of Talland House was the expeditions, in a carriage or by foot, which one could make from there. There are many accounts of visits to Bosigran, Penzance, Land's End and Gurnard's Head.

Local Life

The Stephens did not see themselves as merely visitors but took an active part in activities in the town. They went to the St Ives Arts Club and officiated at many awards ceremonies, being invited to give medals. Leslie Stephen was Vice-President of the Swimming and Sailing Association. Julia continued her philanthropic activities even when on holiday, visiting the sick, sitting on various charitable committees and raising money for a nurse in St Ives. The young Duckworths joined in social events and played in local tennis tournaments. Golf was becoming popular and the *Hyde Park Gate News* records:

On Tuesday Mr George Duckworth accompanied by his younger brother Gerald went to play golf at Lelant. Mr Gerald was easily beaten by Mr George Duckworth. Mr Leslie Stephen with his 3 children walked to Lelant to see the game. . . . On their arrival at Lelant they saw a certain young lady making valiant to hit the golfball which remained untouched while her club flourished wildly in the air some inches above it. Numerous other ladies were playing on account of there being a laidies' match that day. Our correspondent was much struck by the skilful way in which the ladies managed to keep their petticoats down but on the whole he thought the game one which only an energetic man can really enjoy.[10]

In October 1893 Stella donated a guinea to the Prize Fund of the St Ives Board Schools and in the same month Leslie and Julia made one of their many donations of books to the St Ives Free Institute and Library.

Leaving Talland House

The lease of Talland House was eventually sold to the painter Thomas Millie Dow in 1895. Leslie Stephen had been considering selling it for two or three years. He was feeling the financial pressure of paying Thoby's school fees, Gerald and George Duckworth came down less frequently as their work kept them in London, and Laura's mental deterioration meant that she was by now in an institution. Moreover, their pleasure had been diminished when the Porthminster Hotel was built below their house, partly spoiling their view of the bay. What decided the issue, however, was the sudden death of Julia in May 1895. The whole family never went back to St Ives again, though both Vanessa and especially Virginia were to do so many times as adults.

Talland House Today

The town of St Ives has now expanded to surround the originally secluded Talland House. The house has been very much changed since the Stephens left. Thomas Millie Dow built a large extension on the side, which destroys the original symmetry. A plot of land, in the corner of the Talland House garden, was given to Florence Millie Dow's half sister and April Cottage is built there. This was beautifully designed by the architect George Kennedy, who was married to Florence's daughter Mary. There is an interesting connection with Virginia because their nephew Richard Kennedy later became the 'boy at the Hogarth Press', writing his memories of working with Leonard and Virginia Woolf at Hogarth House. Much of the garden has been sold off for development. A car park occupies much of the erstwhile orchard and kitchen garden. The railing round the roof is long gone and the attics extended. The inside was much changed when it was converted into flats in the 1950s. The original staircase from the hallway was ripped out so that now the ground floor is self-contained and access to the upper floors is only from outside. The original fireplaces and other period features and decorations have been removed and new spaces partitioned off. However, the beautiful wrought iron balconies remain and the drawing room and dining room retain their elegant French windows opening out onto steps down to the terrace and garden. One can still imagine the family sitting together in the drawing room or see in the dining room the setting for the dinner party with Mildred's masterpiece, *boeuf en daube*, described in *To the Lighthouse.* Best of all, one can stay at Talland House, stand on the terrace or the balconies and look across the garden with its escallonia hedge, across the Bay, to Godrevy Lighthouse. Virginia Woolf claimed in her novel that the beam shone into their bedrooms and this has been much disputed. However, the light which Vanessa and Virginia saw, which was reputed to be visible at a distance of between fifteen and seventeen miles, was replaced in 1934, so the beam we now see is different.

Godrevy Lighthouse from an upstairs balcony at Talland House, 2002

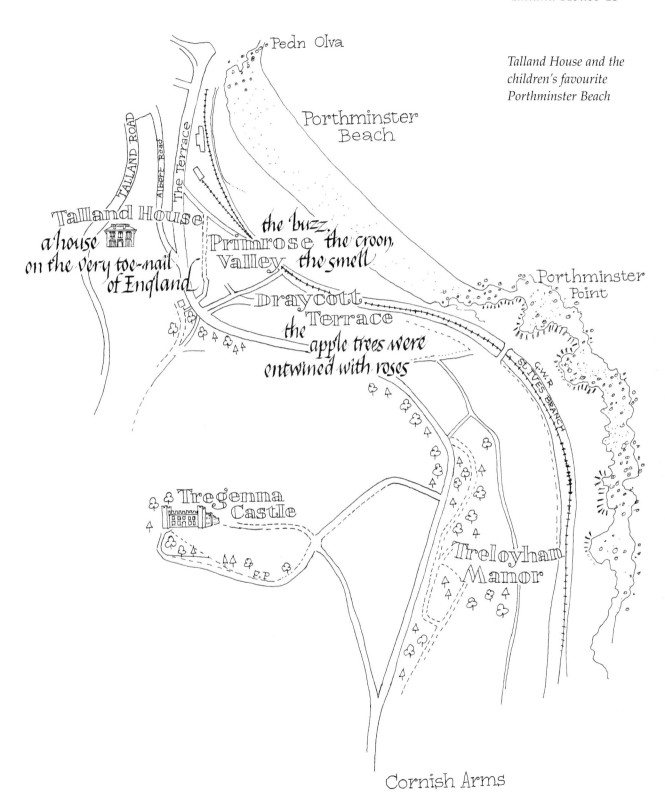

Talland House and the
children's favourite
Porthminster Beach

Pedn Olva

Porthminster
Beach

TALLAND ROAD

Albert Road

The Terrace

Talland House

a house
on the very toe-nail
of England

the buzz.

Primrose
Valley

the croon,

the smell

Draycott
Terrace

the
apple trees were

entwined with roses

Porthminster
Point

G.W.R

ST. IVES BRANCH

Tregenna
Castle

F.P.

Treloyham
Manor

Cornish Arms

*Amy Norris the
seamstress at Talland
House*

*Opposite: A page from Virginia's photograph album
showing a family group at Talland House and two
photographs of the garden. Members of the group are
Leslie Stephen, Lady Albutt, Vanessa, Julia Stephen,
Virginia, Gerald Duckworth, Sir C. Albutt, Adrian
and Shag the dog.*

*Stephen family and
friends studio
photograph taken
at St Ives. Back
row: Mr
Wolstenholme,
Gerald Duckworth.
Middle row:
Arthur Hort, Stella
Duckworth,
Virginia. Front
row: George
Duckworth, Adrian*

L. Stephen. Lady Albutt. Vanessa. JPS. Virginia. Gerald. Sir C Albutt
adrian

ᘒ *Leslie Stephen*

The sea in Cornwall is something quite unlike any English sea that I know -- blue & clear & always with an Oceanic swell breaking against granite cliffs.

Leslie Stephen [1]

Leslie Stephen's love of Cornwall began well before his romance with Talland House and St Ives. Indeed, over a number of years he had walked the length and breadth of Cornwall, and stayed at Falmouth with his first wife Minny in the summer of 1872. Shortly after marrying Julia, Leslie lost no time in introducing her to many parts of Cornwall: his mail was redirected to Post Offices in Bude, Penzance, Falmouth and the Lizard.

Later, when Leslie had found his house and his permanent base, he could indulge his love of the Cornish countryside of West Penwith, the area west of St Ives and towards Land's End, and walk into an ancient landscape, much of it untouched by farming, revealing prehistoric sites, burial chambers, Iron Age hut circles, ancient barrows, stone quoits, an abundance of wild flowers and untried sea cliffs to climb. For several months of the year St Ives became the annual haven for the Stephen family 'in the circle of beautiful children and brilliant intellectuals.' [2]

The Early Days

In the early days of visiting Cornwall, before the building of the branch line to St Ives, Leslie Stephen would have taken the London main line train from Paddington to Penzance, the end of the line. From Penzance he would walk across country and over the moors to Gurnard's Head or Land's End. Perhaps his first view of St Ives was from the coastal path back from Land's End. It would have been a long and arduous journey, leading him to Porthmeor beach, where the surf rolling in from the Atlantic and crashing down on the shore would have thrilled him. Certainly, the journey to Land's End, taking the coast path for most of the way, was one he made frequently, remembering his great friend James Russell Lowell, who used to enjoy visits to St Ives and the walks to Land's End. His friendship with the American diplomat Lowell lasted thirty years.

Leslie Stephen, born in the comfortable area of Kensington, the son of Sir James Stephen and Lady Jane Venn, educated at Eton and Cambridge, and brought up to town life among men of culture and refinement, nevertheless had an affinity with the countryside, rural affairs and the common man. He would rather observe the active lives of the fishermen on the harbour than groan with boredom at talk round the dinner table in London. Leslie was a familiar figure on the harbour; he had been working as editor of the *Cornhill Magazine* from 1871-1882, and

Cliffs and sea pinks

was feeling the freedom of that release. In 1882, that first year in St Ives, he wrote in a letter to George Smith, with whom he was now working as editor on the *Dictionary of National Biography*, 'We are having lovely weather here, and the place is perfectly charming. I think that we have made a great hit in taking the house, which is perfect for our requirements. I shall, I hope, come back ready to write and edit biographies by the dozen.'[3]

Leslie Stephen

Sunday Tramps

In the spring of 1879 Leslie Stephen formed a walking club called The Sunday Tramps. The group of friends would meet at a London railway station, take a short ride and proceed to walk up to twenty miles, taking lunch of bread and cheese in an alehouse along the way. These expeditions often included Cornwall, where he would be exploring new rock climbs. In January 1883 he and his nephew Jem (James Kenneth Stephen) stayed at Talland House without the family. Writing to Julia, he described his walk through Halsetown, Towednack, Amalvear, on to Ding Dong mine and thereby to Land's End. 'We had a glorious day . . . the sea was grand . . . magnificent breakers right over the rocks. . . .' After lunch they walked back, taking in a circle of nine ancient stones known as the Merry Maidens, across country to Penzance and the train ride home to St Ives. He assured Julia that she need not worry about his health, 'considering that I have done pretty well 30 miles today.' Leslie was fifty-one, and one would have thought such a trip very arduous and tiring, but next day they set out for Gurnard's Head:

There we climbed to the top & sat down & had our sandwiches & finished our brandy flask & then I showed him the way down the chimney. I went first . . . his right leg jammed between two rocks . . . the thickest part of him jammed tight also. I had to come at last & try to pick him out like a periwinkle with a pin.[4]

This must be the area's rock climb that Leslie first climbed and recorded for the Alpine Club in 1858 when he was only twenty-six: 'a rock climb gangling and prehensile.' He became editor of the *Alpine Journal* in 1868, a post he held for four years.

However, in spite of the excitement of his climbing and walking adventures and initiating his nephew Jem into the rock climb he wrote to Julia 'Tomorrow I shall be home & St Ives a dream. It seems rather like a dream now; for the absence of you & the little ones make it ghostly.'[5]

Leslie Stephen was among the first rank of Victorian 'Golden Age' mountaineers, and the first climber to record the sport of sea-cliff climbing in Cornwall. He was to be surpassed by Arthur Westlake Andrews, nephew of the Westlakes of Eagle's Nest, Zennor, who were friends of the Stephens. Andrews became known as the Father of Cornish sea-cliff climbing. As a member of the Alpine Club, Leslie Stephen climbed Monte Rosa. He gloried in climbing the Alps and

Botallack Mine, Pendeen

ascended Mont Blanc 'to see the sunset,' writing an account of the event. He was president of the Alpine Club from 1865-'68. Thomas Hardy wrote a poem in 1897, 'The Schreckhorn' (with thoughts of Leslie Stephen), likening Leslie's personality to the mountain.

Leslie's Sunday tramps often included the children, if there were no adults to match him stride for stride across the wild moors. Ten year old Virginia observed 'Mr Stephen who is a renowned pedestrian walked to St Erth in preference to going by locomotive.' She also wrote:

Mr Stephen with his daughter Miss Vanessa Stephen and his son Mr Thoby Stephen went for a walk to Penzance. The real object of the walk was to visit an old British village [Chysauster] which is situated about four miles from Penzance and which takes the walker a little out of his way to visit . . . it is a most venerable and interesting edifice.[6]

Chysauster is an iron-age village of round houses built of stone within a courtyard. Nearer to home there were shorter walks to Carbis Bay (the bay before St Ives), Hawks Point (overlooking Porthkidney beach), Trencrom (an ancient hill-top fort), the Knill Monument (memorial to John Knill, St Ives former Mayor and customs officer), Halsetown (village near St Ives) Zennor (village seven miles west of St Ives) Gurnard's Head (outcrop of rocks beyond Zennor) Bosigran (coastal rocks used by climbers) and Castle-an-Dinas (ancient site and quarry). The whole family would take excursions into the countryside and Julia would organise picnic parties. She especially loved the small beach at Porthcurno with its emerald green sea, where now the open-air Minack theatre perches on the cliffs above. Julia and Leslie would have their own special place on the rocks looking out to sea, at their own local Porthminster beach.

In these first couple of years of owning Talland House, Leslie would often come to St Ives on his own to supervise various improvements that Old Lobb, the gardener and caretaker, would be carrying out. Heather and gorse were planted by the 'tennis ground,' a pond was being dug; a

garden seat for Julia was in place and roses planted to provide a bower. He reported to Julia that the grapes were growing well in their glasshouses, and there would be plenty of potatoes to harvest. However, he missed his wife and having the children, the 'ragamice', around him. One summer visitor to Talland House in 1882, the sister of Walter Sickert, wrote that she 'had the most romantic holiday of my life' with the Stephen family, and described Leslie:

Porthminster beach with seine boats

We had seen his gaunt figure with the ragged red brown beard, striding over the moors, a dog at his heels. He was a formidable man, with an immensely high fore-head, steely-blue eyes and a long pointed nose. We watched with delight his naked babies running about the beach or being towed into the sea between his legs.[7]

In a portrait of Leslie Stephen, as Mr Ramsey, Virginia Woolf allows the artist Lily Briscoe to describe him. 'He is petty, selfish, vain, egotistical; he is spoilt; he is a tyrant; he wears Mrs Ramsay to death; but he has . . . a fiery unworldliness; he knows nothing about trifles; he loves dogs and his children.'[8]

Leonard Woolf felt both Virginia and Vanessa were at times overly critical of their father, a judgement based on knowing all the family:

Having known Leslie Stephen in the flesh and having heard an enormous deal about him from his children, I feel pretty sure that . . . Mr Ramsey [sic] is a pretty good fictional portrait of Leslie Stephen – and yet there are traces of unfairness to Stephen in Ramsey. Leslie Stephen must have been in many ways an exasperating man within the family and he exasperated his daughters, particularly Vanessa.[9]

Leslie Stephen was so much in love with Cornwall that he wanted to share his pleasure with friends. In July 1884 he wrote to Mrs W.K. Clifford:

We are here on a lovely blowing breezy day: the air is delicious – pure Atlantic breezes . . . and it is as soft as silk; it has a fresh sweet taste like new milk; and it is so clear that we see thirty miles of coast. We have gardens each full of romance for the children – lawns surrounded by flowering hedges, and intricate thickets of gooseberries and currants, and remote nooks of potatoes and peas, and high banks altogether a pocket-paradise with a sheltered cove of sand in easy reach (for 'Ginia even) just below.

Also there is a railway station between us and the said cove . . . you must come here when we go . . . it is a sin to leave the place to itself for so long and it would be an unadulterated pleasure to think of you and your little ones getting some good out of it. The effect is at present to make me so sleepy and lazy that I am exhausted even by writing this.[10]

Mrs Lucy Clifford did indeed take Talland House for a few months, with her two daughters and an aunt. Leslie told Julia, on one of his lone visits during their occupancy, that the house looked very comfortable. There was a new writing table for the drawing room, which had been bought at Penzance.

The Ragamice

The Ragamice was Leslie's pet name for his youngest children, Vanessa, Thoby, Virginia, and Adrian. Laura, an older child from his first marriage, was proving a difficult child to manage, and she was soon put into a home for the mentally deficient. But in the early days Leslie had hopes for her. While in St Ives negotiating the lease for Talland House, he wrote to Julia and slipped in a note for eleven year old Laura:

My darling Laura, I am in a beautiful place called St Ives. We shall come in the summer I hope. There is a beautiful beach for the little ones. You will bathe there and learn to swim. . . . It is a very nice house, with a garden and a fountain and grapes and strawberries and peaches. I hope that you have been good. It makes me very unhappy if mother tells me you have been naughty. Your loving father.[11]

At Talland House Leslie involved himself in the children's games and their education. He enjoyed their activities: 'Yesterday we went to Trencrom. The children had their inevitable nets: for they are quite mad about bugs.'[12] He wrote to his friend Norton about his holiday, and Thoby who, 'rising five, produced a box which he called his "contradictionary box" and gave as a reason for the name that it was full of rubbish. What muddled notions had got into his little noddle I cannot imagine . . .'[13] 'Father & the three [Thoby, Virginia and Adrian] sailed after lunch with old Roach. Mother, Nessa & I went to Hain['s].'[14]

Virginia held a special place in Leslie's heart. It was she who raided his library for books and satisfied his need for admiration and affection. Virginia could charm her father and play the coquette with impunity. In 1883 writing to Julia who was away, Leslie reported the daily happenings:

Little Ginia is already an accomplished flirt. I said today that I must go down to my work. She nestled herself down on the sofa by me; squeezed her little self tightly up against me and then gazed up with her bright eyes through her shock of hair and said "Don't go, Papa!" She looked full of mischief all the time. I never saw such a little rogue.[15]

With his eldest son Thoby, he was prepared to show a playful authority 'I hope that you have not kicked Nessa out of bed again. If you do, I shall have to kick you out of the window – and you might be hurt. Kisses to Nessa, Ginia and Adrian.'[16]

Leslie was often away visiting literary friends, tramping the country-side or engaging in some mountain climb. In 1893, Leslie wrote to Vanessa from a climbing expedition in Switzerland:

Darling Nessa, How does the typewriting get on? Shall you be ready to write all my articles when I get home? We are almost snowed up; but it has left off snowing now. It has spoilt all the tobogganing and skating. I shall be glad to get home to my little girl & see what a number of sums she has done. Yr loving father LS [17]

Whether Vanessa became a competent typist or not, it is clear that her developing interest in art was becoming important. One year on and her father is pleased that someone has shown an interest in Vanessa and spoken well of her drawing. 'I shall truly be glad if she has a talent that way.' Although Leslie had no particular interest in painting, as long as Vanessa took her work seriously, he was prepared to offer all the help he could. In *The Mausoleum Book,* written for his children after the death of their mother, he wrote 'I have always been shy with artistic people, who inhabit a world very unfamiliar to me.'[18] His approval of his daughter's interest in art is therefore admirable, and the fact that he would accompany the children willingly to art exhibitions. 'Us four Stella & father went to the National Portrait Gallery.'[19]

Artists and Writers

Leslie Stephen wrote to his friend Charles Norton in America that St Ives attracted him more than ever:

We have even made a pleasant acquaintance with some of the school of artists wh. has strangely sprung up here within the last three or four years. We have even a little picture gallery! One of them is a Yankee named Simmons who once attend-

ed your lectures & is married to a lovely Californian. Another is one Adrian Stokes, who sells pictures now for good prices & has an Austrian wife. [20]

Edward E. Simmons's wife Vesta, and Marianne Stokes, were painters in their own right. James Lanham established the art gallery in 1887, with the help of members of the Arts Club, and Vanessa, at ten years of age would have seen the work of these artists hanging in the gallery, and met them while she purchased her own materials for drawing and painting in Lanham's art shop.

That Leslie Stephen was aware of developments in the artists' community is evidence that the Stephen family were indeed familiar with the artists and the Arts Club activities. In 1892 we have Virginia reporting that 'The St Ives Mrs Simmons came to luncheon. She gave Miss Vanessa Stephen a tie which was not duly appreciated.'[21] The gift was a present for Vanessa's birthday. The Simmons lived at 23 The Terrace. Another member of the Arts Club was Bosch-Reitz who painted a portrait of Leslie that was hung in the Royal Academy Summer Exhibition of 1890. *The Spectator* reported

There is one other capital portrait in the Gallery . . . it is a head of Mr Leslie Stephen. It is pleasant to record this association of Art and Literature in the persons of Mr Bosch-Reitz, the popular St Ives artist, and his subject, Mr Leslie Stephen, who from long residence may almost be claimed a St Ives man. [22]

Leslie attracted many prominent members of the literary world who desired to visit him. In 1884 and 1886 the American novelist Henry James was lodging near by at the Tregenna Castle Hotel. The critic Edmund Gosse and his wife Nellie were staying at the same hotel in 1890. He wrote 'We went to St Ives to be near Leslie Stephen, with whom I took immense walks of a wholly speechless character. He and I went to the wrestling at Redruth I remember.'[23] Stella recorded in her diary 'Father & Georgie went off by 11 o'clock train to Truro to see wrestling. . . . The wrestlers returned at 7 having had a good time.'[24] The writer George

Meredith, friend and fellow Sunday Tramp, was several times a guest at Talland House or Tregenna Castle and at 8 Belmont Terrace, St Ives. In 1892 Mrs Holman Hunt was staying with a party at 5 The Terrace. F.W. Maitland, fellow Sunday Tramp and writer of the first biography of Leslie in 1906, was a frequent visitor at St Ives and Hyde Park Gate.

St Ives Arts Club

In 1890 Mr and Mrs Stephen, prominent members of St Ives society and well-qualified for the St Ives Arts Club, were invited to join it. The rules said 'Only Professional Painters, Engravers, Sculptors, Architects, Authors and Musicians, resident in or visiting St Ives and their wives, husbands and relations, shall be eligible for membership.' At a meeting of the Club the secretary read a letter from Leslie Stephen, on behalf of

Borlase Smart with his painting of the Arts Club

himself and Mrs Stephen, accepting the invitation to membership. Of the hundred members, they were among the first to join, closely followed by Mr and Mrs Stanhope Forbes, artists from Newlyn, along with people from other professions. Mr Hain, the ship owner, and Mrs Hain were brought as guests of Julius Olsson in this first year.

The novelist Compton Mackenzie, who wrote pantomimes for the Arts Club stage and whose sister Fay, the actress, performed in them, was introduced to the Club by the writer Charles Marriott. Mackenzie, in his autobiography *My Life and Times*, recalled Leslie Stephen entertaining a large gathering at Talland House, and that he would act as editor for a number of writers who gave their manuscripts to him to read for his opinion, before submitting them for publication.

Charles Marriott

Charles Marriott knew many writers and artists, among them W.H. Hudson, the naturalist writer; Dr Havelock Ellis, sexual psychologist; Ranger Gull, who wrote under the pseudonym Guy Thorne; and Bernard Walke, vicar of St Hilary, and his artist wife Annie. Marriott invited Hugh Walpole to stay at their house on Porthminster Terrace, where he encouraged his first attempt at a novel, *The Wooden Horse*. E.M. Forster had praised it but Compton Mackenzie, living at Hayle near St Ives, declared that Walpole wasn't really a novelist and was then rather upset when his novel was published in 1909, before his own first novel, *The Passionate Elopement*. Mackenzie's second novel *Carnival* was filmed in Cornwall and *Whisky Galore* was inspired by Cornwall.

Later, Hugh Walpole and Virginia Woolf exchanged opinions on various writers of the day.

In 1891 Leslie Stephen was elected President of the Arts Club. It is

Arts Club members - a Saturday night, 1895

likely that his friend Adrian Stokes, the Arts Club's first president, proposed him but he did not take office because of ill health and therefore, sadly, his name is not written on the roll of past Presidents. He suffered a serious breakdown in 1889, which recurred in 1891, causing him to resign his editorship of the *Dictionary of National Biography*, a task that had engaged him from 1882, much of it written in St Ives. Mrs Stephen wrote to his fellow editor, George Smith: 'He has no idea how very serious and complicated his illness has been, though I think he acknowledges now that for some time the strain has been too great for him '[25]

However, that same year, and probably because of his work on the Dictionary, he was made an Honorary Doctor of Letters at Cambridge. He did not neglect his civic duties even when his health broke down. In 1892 he was elected President of the London Library, and in 1894 his literary interests were sufficient to persuade him to preside at the annual dinner of the Society of Authors in London.

A St Ives Man

Leslie Stephen and his family were part of the town of St Ives and they took an interest in events, whether it was in socialising with friends, or mixing with the local inhabitants and involving themselves in the general welfare of the town. Swimming was a great sport in St Ives and every year on Regatta Day championship races of boating and swimming took place in the harbour. There was a carnival atmosphere, and decorations and flags and brass bands celebrated the event.

Leslie Stephen was considered to be a 'St Ives man.' Certainly the Stephens were more involved in local affairs than is generally known. In the General Election of 1892 Mr Bedford Bolitho, MP visited St Ives to address a meeting at the Public Hall. It was presided over by Leslie Stephen, who said he was very glad to have a share with his fellow townsmen in discharging an important political duty. Mrs Julia Stephen and Miss Stella Duckworth were noted in the audience. Mr and Mrs Bolitho were among the visitors at Talland House.

Are you Ready?
Painting by W.H. Bartlett c.1900

Sporting Activities

The artists in St Ives were responsible for setting up many sporting societies. The Arts Club President Adrian Stokes and a committee of five other artists established the West Cornwall Golf Club in 1889, with links on Lelant Towans overlooking Porthkidney sands, and running beside the branch line to St Ives. The following year Arthur Conan Doyle, whose stories of Sherlock Holmes were being published in the *Strand Magazine*, was a visiting player. The Lawn Tennis Club was refereed by the artist W.H.Y. Titcomb, responsible for a number of paintings of local fisher families. In 1890 Jack Hills, Stella's future husband, was teamed with George Duckworth to play against Gerald H. Duckworth and Edward E. Simmons, the American painter.

An artists' cricket team

The Cricket Club, too, was captained by Adrian Stokes, with a team of local artists. Cricket was a favourite sport for competition between the Newlyn and St Ives artists, culminating in a yearly match. There were also the matches played with Town and Visitors v. Artists. In 1889 the recorded score was Artists 37 runs, Town 19. It may have been this very match that Leslie Stephen referred to in a letter to his American friend Charles Eliot Norton in September 1889. His son Rupert Norton had been staying with them at Talland House. 'They [George and Gerald] have taught him to play cricket among other things & on Friday he performed in a match against the town of St Ives.'[26]

On one of Leslie's return trips to London he recalled a young man on the train, an artist, 'one of the St Ives eleven & he described the accident at the match. One of the colliders got a concussion of the brain & is not yet recovered.'[27] The match was the annual event between Newlyn and

St Ives. The artist with concussion, playing for the Newlyn team, was Fred Millard. A doctor was called to the scene, and afterwards Edward E Simmons, of the local team, looked after him at his home until accommodation could be found in St Ives. Stanhope Forbes wrote of the rivalry between St Ives and Newlyn: 'Oh it was nothing to do with painting, or art of any kind; it was much more serious, for it concerned cricket.'[28]

One prominent artist, Julius Olsson, played an active role in local affairs over a period of twenty years, becoming a Justice of the Peace. In writing of his memories years later, he stated

There is no place in England of the size of St Ives that has had such a marked influence on the progress of British Art during the last forty years. It has been visited by so many people, distinguished in art and literature. One of my earliest recollections was dining with Leslie Stephen at Talland House. . . . St Ives materially helped me in my art and I am grateful for it.[29]

Vanessa's Responsibilities

Of the four younger children of Julia Stephen Vanessa, being the eldest girl, and probably more conscious of her mother's caring ways than her younger siblings, was closest to her mother. To Leslie, Julia's death was a devastating blow, tinged with feelings of guilt. 'In the hideous morbid dreams wh. came to me, I could not escape from self-reproaches – perhaps not all unjust – that I had not made my love clearer.'[30]

In August he wrote from Freshwater, Isle of Wight, to tell his friend Charles Norton 'I should have liked to go to St Ives. The associations with her would no doubt bring pain but it is a kind of pain wh. I should not regret.'[31] However, it was already decided to part with Talland House before Julia's death, because of the difficulties of travel and for financial reasons.

Leslie's remaining years were a trial to Vanessa. Both her mother and Stella had been ideal models of womanhood whose foremost duties were service to the family and fulfilling the expectations of a Victorian father. He was in his sixties when Vanessa, at eighteen years, was forced to assume household responsibilities. 'My Vanessa is taking her place as mistress of the house very calmly & will be invaluable.'[32]

Vanessa had much less in common with her father than Virginia. Leslie took a bully's delight in terrifying Vanessa over the household accounts, as though punishing her for not being her mother or Stella, but summer visitors to Talland House, and especially their cousin Herbert Fisher, had a different view: 'Leslie, so formidable within the home, was a different creature when he was striding over the Cornish cliffs, botanizing as he went, repeating poetry, and overflowing with good spirits and enjoyment. I learnt to know him from these St Ives visits and always held him in deep affection and regard.'[33]

However, Julia must have suffered from his penny-pinching ways for he wrote in earlier letters, almost by way of apology, 'I have been making up my mind not to care any more about money.'[34] Money, Julia and the family were clearly matters which concerned him: 'I do feel that you and the mites are everything to me. My one discomfort (money is only a passing irritation to me) is to see you looking so worn & to feel, as I feel oftener than you imagine – that it is my fault that I don't make you happier.'[35]

The Last Years

After Julia's death Leslie's responsibilities must have rested heavily on him, yet he did not farm his children out to various relatives, as many fathers would have done at that time, and he had more than a justifiable excuse because of his advancing age:

My one plain duty & my one hope of regaining a tolerable state of mind is to do all I can for her children. I must devote myself absolutely to that: must teach the girls & be with the boys on their holidays & keep up the bonds which unite me to the older children. They are all I could wish to me; but I feel it essential to keep them as close as I can. . . . I have let St Ives, as indeed, she & I had already meant to do for many reasons.[36]

It is true that Leslie Stephen's family was vital to him. His interest in their affairs was paramount. He relies on his children to give him 'something like life again'. He was cheered by the family in their hold on life and was anxious to get back to normal living. He wrote to a friend that all the children were well; Thoby was enjoying Cambridge, Vanessa her studio and Virginia engrossed in literary papers.

In the last few years of his life he gained many honours from Oxford and Cambridge, Edinburgh and Harvard Universities, and several historical and antiquary societies. He was appointed a Trustee of the National Portrait Gallery but was forced to resign when his deafness made meetings pointless. His final accolade was in 1902 when he was made a KCB, Knight Commander of the Order of the Bath.

Vanessa's last few years with her father were made more stressful by his being deaf. He wanted to be involved with his children, his ragamice, and not be neglected in any of their affairs. His complaints were pitiful. After his death it is no wonder Vanessa felt some relief, and release, from these responsibilities.

Sir Leslie Stephen died in February, 1904. The Cornish *Western Echo*, quoting from *The Times*, described him:

The distinguished essayist and first editor of the Dictionary of National Biography died on Monday at his residence in London. He was the son of the late Sir James Stephen and brother of the late Sir James Fitzjames Stephen, Judge of the High Court. He was one of the foremost men of letters of his age. . . . He came to fill the first place in the literary world of his day. He spent a considerable amount of time in St Ives . . .[37]

Frederick Maitland, related to the family by marriage, wrote the first biography of Leslie Stephen, summing up those painful last few years: 'The blue eyes wander round appealingly from child to child, for he cannot hear what they are saying, and wants to know why they are laughing. The little joke, or whatever it is, must be shouted into his ear or he will not be content.'[38]

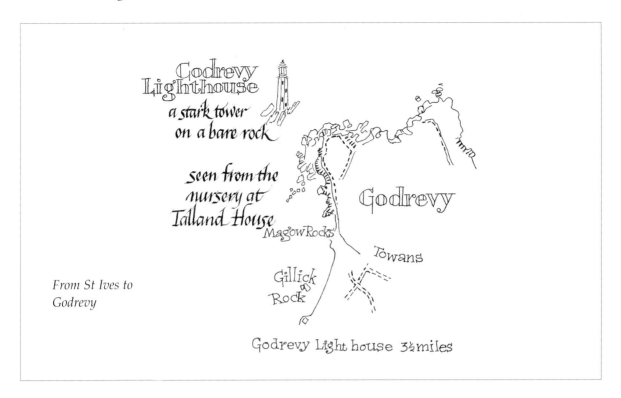

Godrevy Lighthouse
a stark tower
on a bare rock

seen from the
nursery at
Talland House

Godrevy

Magow Rocks

Towans

*From St Ives to
Godrevy*

Gillick
Rock

Godrevy Light house 3½ miles

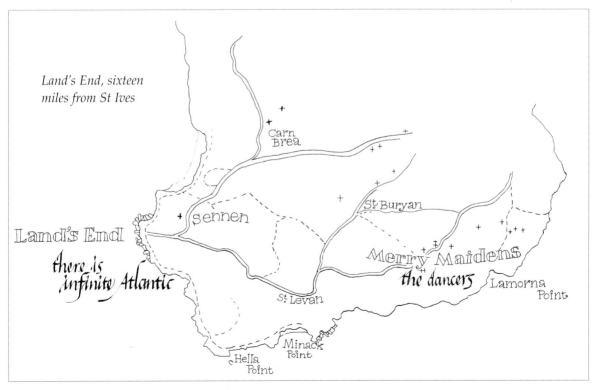

*Land's End, sixteen
miles from St Ives*

Carn
Brea

St Buryan

Land's End

Sennen

Merry Maidens

there is
infinite Atlantic

the dancers

Lamorna
Point

St Levan

Minack
Point

Hella
Point

✐ *Julia Stephen*

When I look at certain little photographs - at one in which I am reading by her side at St Ives with Virginia in the background . . . I see as with my bodily eyes the love, the holy and tender love which breathes through those exquisite lips, and I know that the later years were a deep strong current of calm inward happiness, and the trials, so to speak, merely floating accidents on the surface.

Leslie Stephen [1]

Julia Duckworth Stephen is surrounded by a number of romantic and bizarre stories, with a colourful background completely at odds with that of Leslie Stephen. She was born in India and educated for some of her childhood in Paris, living for a while at Versailles. Her mother was one of the famously beautiful but unconventional Pattle sisters. As a young woman, Julia herself was noted for her ethereal, Pre-Raphaelite beauty. She was a model for the painters Burne-Jones, Holman Hunt and Watts, as well as for her aunt, the famous and eccentric Victorian photographer Julia Margaret Cameron. Another aunt was Sarah Prinsep, who lived at Little Holland House, surrounding herself with well known and well connected artists, writers, dignitaries and politicians of the day. As a young woman Julia was often part of this lively, fashionable, social circle.

Virginia with her parents Leslie and Julia Stephen, in the drawing room at Talland House. 1893

First Marriage

She met her first husband, Herbert Duckworth, while in Venice as nurse companion to her invalid mother. She was married at the age of twenty-one and by all accounts their marriage was romantic, loving and intensely happy. George Duckworth was born just ten months after their marriage and Stella about fifteen months after that. Then disaster struck. While they were staying with Julia's sister Adeline and her husband

Julia Stephen photographed by her aunt, Julia Margaret Cameron. 1872

Henry Vaughan, Herbert Duckworth died suddenly and bizarrely of a burst abscess after reaching up to pick a fig for her. Julia was left with her two babies while heavily pregnant with Gerald, who was born just six weeks after his father's death. She spent much time recuperating with her aunt Julia Margaret Cameron at her home, Dimbola, at Freshwater on the Isle of Wight. In 1875 she moved into 13 Hyde Park Gate South. A few months later the newly widowed Leslie Stephen moved into the house next door with his young daughter Laura, and his sister-in-law Anny Thackeray. Julia and Leslie already knew each other. She had been friendly with both him and his wife Minny, and with her sister Anny, who lived with them. Julia had already helped the distraught widower, especially with practical advice about his daughter Laura, who was only five, the same age as Gerald. Now that they lived so close she was able to do so more and more, and Leslie increasingly applied to her for advice and guidance.

The Red Dress *painted by Vanessa in 1929, from a photograph of her mother*

Marriage to Leslie Stephen

After a reluctant and often strange courtship, Julia finally consented to marry Leslie and a quiet ceremony took place on March 26th, 1878. Leslie and Laura moved into Julia's house, which was later renumbered 22 Hyde Park Gate, and remained their home till Leslie's death and the Stephen children's move to Bloomsbury. It must have been a time of great adjustment and a severe test and drain on Julia's strength. Suddenly there were four children in the household, and fourteen months later Vanessa was born, on May 30th, 1879, followed just over a year after that by Thoby on September 8th, 1880. It was soon after this that Leslie Stephen discovered Talland House and thought it an attractive holiday home for his rapidly expanding family. He and Julia had already spent the summer of 1879 very happily in Cornwall, at Newquay, while she was recuperating after Vanessa's difficult birth. Both loved the area. By the time they first went

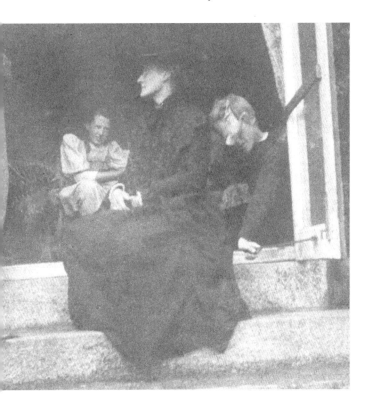

Julia Stephen with Virginia and Adrian at the drawing room window. 1890s

together to Talland House in the summer of 1882 Virginia had also been born and in October 1883 came Adrian. Julia had had three children in just over three years before she was widowed at twenty-four. In her second marriage she had four more children in just over four years, the last when she was thirty-seven, dangerously old to be giving birth in those days, and, according to Virginia, in spite of taking precautions. In between, Julia had helped nurse her dying father and sister as well as other close relations and friends. Her mother, Mrs Jackson, also demanded almost constant nursing care and attention, though she finally died only two years before Julia herself. She had looked after a difficult step-daughter, Laura, who was eventually put into a home and then an asylum. She had to look after and support Leslie, who was in many ways the most demanding of all, with what Virginia called, 'a godlike, yet childlike, standing in the family.'[2] Julia must have been continuously emotionally and physically exhausted, and while no doubt she looked forward immensely to her Cornish summers, they were not in fact a respite from work and caring.

Talland House

From the first she, too, loved the house and their holiday life at Talland House, though it must also have given her many additional burdens. The logistics of getting a large, young family with all the luggage and servants down to St Ives from London devolved almost solely on her. Several times Leslie decided to walk part of the way to Cornwall for his own pleasure and exercise, consciously avoiding getting into what he called 'tantarums' and abandoning everything to Julia to arrange. Once there, it would be up to her to make sure that the house ran smoothly, that local help was hired and efficient, and that food and rooms were ready for the family and their many guests throughout the summer. This she appears to have managed with cheerful efficiency, and many accounts attest to her serenity and her skill in defusing tension and reconciling conflicts.

It was her laughter, her unusual turn of phrase and her ability to tell amusing anecdotes that Virginia most remembered about her. She was noted for her ability to draw out shy guests and make sure they were included in activities. When Leslie, bored or irritated, simply withdrew from the company by 'plunging' into his back den, or paced backwards and forwards along the terrace, she was left to smooth over the resulting awkwardness. She could also calm the often-tempestuous Leslie, and possibly this would be easier for her than in London as he would be more relaxed, loving the opportunity for long walks and talk with interesting friends.

Julia's Life at Talland House

One of the best accounts of Julia at Talland House is that by Leslie in his *Mausoleum Book*, the threnody which he composed to pass on his memories to his children. He claimed that his pleasantest memories were all during their summers at Talland House. He emphasises Julia's love of the garden: 'I can see my Julia strolling among her beloved flowers: sitting in the "loo corner", a sheltered seat behind the grape-house, or the so-called "coffee garden", where on hot days she would be shaded by the great escallonia hedge; and, still oftener, in the porch from which we used to watch the cricket.'[3]

Virginia also remembered her mother sitting knitting in the porch while she watched cricket or other games. It could be a dangerous place, however; both Stella and Margaret Lushington record in their diaries how, when Walter Headlam missed a catch from Gerald, the ball landed instead on Julia's head, causing slight concussion and necessitating a visit from Dr Nicholls.

Julia spent much time with her children, watching their games, reading to them, or gossiping with the older ones. She encouraged their hobbies, especially photography, once insisting that a reluctant Sophie, the cook, allow herself to be photographed by Gerald. She allowed them to have their pets and their collections of shells, seaweed, pieces of bone, butterflies and moths, though she apparently drew the line at caterpillars in the house in case they got squashed underfoot. She would even go to one of the public houses in St Ives to buy rum for their moth collecting, usually accompanied by a young male guest. Virginia in particular felt very close to her mother and her earliest memories are all of St Ives. She remembered her mother on the bedroom balcony surrounded by passion flowers, or sitting at the dining room table under the portrait of Beatrice, which had been given to her by her governess. Julia, however, probably felt closest to Adrian, her baby. Possibly because she felt

Julia in the garden at Talland House, c.1894

excluded, Virginia later explored the mother-son relationship as harmfully over-protective in a number of her novels.

Leslie Stephen liked Mrs Jackson, Julia's mother, who often stayed with them. She spent a particularly long time with them during the hot summer of 1887 when Leslie remembered mother and daughter sitting under the trees by the tennis lawn, listening to George Meredith reading his poetry. He remembered, too, her love of expeditions, her favourites to Porthcurno, Gurnard's Head or Bosigran Castle:

She was an admirable conductor of such expeditions, catering with unimpeachable skill in the department of provisions, and keeping everyone in good temper. The sun of those dear summer days still seems to shine for me. They are associated with some of our best friends, above all with Lowell. Lowell loved our scenery; but neither he nor anyone enjoyed it more than my Julia. I can feel her sitting by me on the rocky point which bounds Porthminster Bay, watching the seagulls in whom she delighted, or on the rocks by Knill's monument – a favourite haunt of hers and Lowell's. Ah, those days were full of happiness! [4]

Often though, especially when the children were very young, Julia stayed in the garden when the others were going on long expeditions, or took her babies to play on Porthminster Beach. The *Hyde Park Gate News* for August 1st, 1892 records an episode when Julia and Laura were left at Carbis Bay while the others walked further on to Hawks Point. Here Miss Vanessa Stephen was 'enough lacking in common sense' as to leave behind Julia's umbrella. This apparently happened so often that it was a source of teasing by her family. Julia did, of course, have a lot of help with the younger children, both from maids and governesses and from the older Duckworth children, especially Stella, and their friends. This enabled her to pursue her own affairs in the town and to go on what they called 'botanising' walks with Leslie. Virginia, Vanessa, Stella and other family members and friends all record in letters, memoirs and diaries the same happy memories of Talland House with Julia as its central presence.

Vanessa Stephen and Lisa Stillman at Talland House, c. Aug. 1892

*A photograph by H.H. Hay-Cameron of a drawing of Julia Stephen
by Lisa Stillman inscribed 'S to S 1893'*

Stories for Children

Julia loved telling stories and she made up her own for her children. She set them in locations they knew and loved, either in London or St Ives, and they are full of personal details which would have amused and involved them. They provide a fascinating insight into Julia's relationship with her children. The main characters, often the only characters, are talking animals. In 1885 she and Leslie negotiated unsuccessfully with Routledge about publication. Julia had already written *Agnostic Women* and an entry for the *Dictionary of National Biography* on her aunt Julia Margaret Cameron. She had also had *Notes from Sickrooms* published by Smith Elder and Co. Her *Stories for Children*, with illustrations by Leslie and Vanessa, were only finally published, however, a century later in 1987. It is suggested that Leslie Stephen's drawings were idle doodlings, not originally meant to accompany the stories, but there must surely have been some collaboration. It cannot have been coincidental that she wrote about, and he drew, a monkey smoking a pipe or riding on a goat. Vanessa later took one of her mother's stories, 'Emlycaunt', and stitched her own illustrations into appropriate places in the text.

The stories, with long stilted conversations, strike a modern reader as dated, but they lack the heavy didacticism and morality associated with most Victorian fiction for children, possibly because of Julia's atheism. The message, if there is one, is about being kind to animals. There are two stories set in an unnamed, but clearly recognisable, St Ives. In 'The Monkey on the Moor' the children stay each summer in a 'funny little fishing town stretching out into the sea, the houses all so crowded together. . . .'[5] Their house is a little outside the town. They play on the beach all day, catching fish and crabs and collecting shells to take back to London. In the evenings they play in the little sloping garden with a fountain in one corner and their playground in the other. Further away is the moor, thickly carpeted with heather and golden gorse, with rocky outcrops of grey stone, where the animals meet at the Quoit.

The main character, Jocko a monkey, is surely inspired by Thoby's toy monkey, Jacko. When Thoby was away at boarding school, Vanessa, who missed her brother horribly, used to take Jacko to bed with her. This same story includes an account of a naughty little girl called Ginia who buries her shoes and socks in the sand when playing on the beach and has to be carried back home barefoot. Next day her mother takes her into the town to buy new shoes. There seems to be no diary or memoir reference showing that this event actually happened, but it rings true.

The Lanyon Quoit

Julia has obviously drawn on her 'botanising' walks with Leslie for close observation of the topography and the colours, sounds and habitats of wildlife, especially birds: 'The seagull went softly up into the air, then came down on the crest of a wave, her grey and white feathers shining like silver in the sun. Then a gannet rose high and straight and like a sail splashed deep through the clear green water, and in a second she was up again with a struggling silvery fish in her strong beak.' [6]

In 'The Wandering Pigs'

Three pigs lived in a very comfortable home near the sea. The cliffs which rose up from the beach were covered with short sweet grass with here and there a tuft of pale pink thrift. In the spring the harebells and yellow poppies bloomed and the bees came humming by. There was a house near and a sheltered garden full of roses and raspberries, in the corner of which stood a row of yellow beehives. The garden was cut out of the side of the cliff and when Aubrey and Conor came up from the beach by the little winding path, they used to stand on the top of the broad stone wall and look down on the yellow roses which grew in a tangled mass on the old apple tree. . . .[7]

Julia's young listeners would instantly recognise this as Primrose Valley and their path to and from Porthminster Beach. There is a strange but appealing mixture of local detail, close observation and anthropomorphism. As well as talking pigs, porpoises, bears, various other animals and birds, and 'lovely Vanessa butterflies '[8], 'a dragonfly darted past with his glistening wings lighting up the dark corners where the lazy water gnats stretched their long useless legs on the surface of the pool.'[9] There are fishermen in blue jerseys, fishing-boats with brown sails, and 'a long pier which ran out to sea and far off, rising straight out of the sea, was a white lighthouse on whose windows the sun was burning fiercely. On the pier was a monkey painting.'[10]

Mrs Ramsay

Virginia Woolf articulated the complex relationship between her parents, and between herself and her parents, in her highly autobiographical novel, *To the Lighthouse*, where Julia is only barely fictionalised as Mrs Ramsay. Vanessa wrote to her sister when the novel was published and attested to the accuracy of the portrayal:

you have given a portrait of mother which is more like her to me than anything I could ever have conceived possible. It is almost painful to have her so raised from the dead. You have made one feel the extraordinary beauty of her character, which must be the most difficult thing in the world to do. It was like meeting her again with oneself grown up and on equal terms and it seems to me the most astonishing feat of creation to have been able to see her in such a way. You have given father too I think as clearly, but perhaps, I may be wrong, that isn't quite so difficult. There is more to catch hold of. Still it seems to me to be the only thing about him which ever gave a true idea.[11]

Virginia felt that the experience had been highly cathartic for her. She claimed to have been 'obsessed' by her mother from her death when she was thirteen to when she was forty-four and wrote *To the Lighthouse*. 'When it was written, I ceased to be obsessed by my mother. I no longer hear her voice; I do not see her. I suppose that I did for myself what psycho-analysts do for their patients.'[12]

Mrs Ramsay knits together all aspects of the family and the novel, both literally with her constant knitting of the stockings for the lighthouse keeper's son, and figuratively. The rhythms of the language that represent her are fluid, inclusive and expansive. Her expressions are often exaggerated. Conversely Mr Ramsay is represented as reductive, limiting and disruptive. Mrs Ramsay, like Julia, is shown as attentive to the undercurrents of family life and relationships. She anticipates reactions and is anxious to avoid people feeling left out or hurt, often by giving them special pieces of food or little attentions. She is concerned about matchmaking. She is outside masculine discussions about square roots of numbers, the Waverley novels, or students' dissertations. She watches a speaker's manner to understand how they are feeling, rather than listening to the content of their speech. The representation of the ebb and flow of feeling and conversations in the famous dinner party scene seems very accurately portrayed. Julia's love for her children and her ability to solve apparently irreconcilable disputes comes through strongly in the episode where Mrs Ramsay covers up the skull nailed to the nursery wall. James refuses to have it moved and moreover needs a nightlight. Cam has nightmares because of the huge shadows of bones on the wall. Mrs Ramsay calms Cam's fears by covering the skull with her shawl and then sitting with her, talking softly till she is asleep. Turning to James, she assures him the skull will remain there and that they will go to the Lighthouse, though not the following day. He too goes happily to sleep.

Virginia's portrait of her mother as Mrs Ramsay is not, however, altogether positive or uncritical. Like all else in the novel it is unstable; there are many conflicting perspectives and opinions. Lily Briscoe recognises that even fifty pairs of eyes, each with different perspectives, would not be enough to make sense of such a complex character. All Mrs Ramsay's virtues can also be seen as vices. Her matchmaking, for instance, can be seen as caring and empathetic but conversely as intrusive and manipulative. Virginia felt very strongly that she especially, and the family in general, were neglected and sacrificed to Julia's devotion to Leslie and to her philanthropic works. With bitter irony she wrote that 'for many years she made a fetish of his health; and so . . . she wore herself out and died at forty-nine; while he lived on, and found it very difficult, so healthy was he, to die of cancer at the age of seventy-two.'[13]

However, Virginia's response to her parents and assessment of their personalities, changed through her writing life. 'Reminiscences', written about 1907, is an apprentice piece aimed at an audience of her sister, family and close friends, and apparently not intended for publication. It exhibits the bitterness and sense of betrayal she felt, that her mother should have died and left her. 'A Sketch of the Past', a memoir read to friends in 1939 and later published, is, as one would expect, much more mature, considered and reflective. Distance and her own life experiences have softened her judgements of both her parents. She acknowledges that the present affects the way one writes about the past. Her essay about her father written in 1932 is also more mellow and positive.

The Angel in the House

By the time she wrote *To the Lighthouse*, which was published in 1927, Virginia Woolf was well aware of the problems of reconciling a woman's role as wife and mother with the demands of an artistic life. She gave a lecture on January 21st, 1931, which was later published, called *Professions for Women*. In this she argued that a woman could only be a writer, or fully pursue any form of creative and artistic life, if she first 'killed the Angel in the House'. The Angel in the House was the iconic Victorian role for a woman, canonised as the perfect wife and mother. It is precisely the image of Julia constructed by Leslie Stephen in his *Mausoleum Book*. The term comes from a long poem by Coventry Patmore. Patmore had been a close friend of Julia's mother, Mrs Jackson, and Julia herself had a copy of the poem inscribed by the author.

Virginia defines the Angel as intensely sympathetic, immensely charming, and utterly unselfish. With powerful irony she then subverts such apparently laudable virtues: the Angel 'excelled in the difficult arts of family life. She sacrificed herself daily. If there was chicken, she took the leg; if there was a draught she sat in it.'[14] Her beauty is emphasised but it can be seen as manipulative. Leonard Woolf later mischievously disparaged the melancholy perfection of Julia's beauty, as represented in many portraits, as 'saintly dying duck loveliness.'[15] Stella, Vanessa and Virginia were all being groomed by Julia to take over this sacrificial role. Stella's own early death, only three months after her marriage to Jack Hills, means that we cannot assess how far she would accept that role, though all accounts suggest it would have been much as her mother would have planned. Vanessa and Virginia were only saved from what they saw as the tyrannies of having to preside at the ceremonial tea-table and the rigours of polite society to which their step-brother, George, tried to introduce them, by the deaths of their parents and their escape to Bloomsbury. In *To the Lighthouse* Virginia kills off Mrs Ramsay, the Angel in the House, and allows the future to belong to the artist Lily Briscoe, who contains much of both herself and Vanessa. Significantly, Virginia and Leonard Woolf chose to publish the novel, through their Hogarth Press, on May 5th, the anniversary of Julia's death.

Caring for the Sick and the Poor

Even on holiday at Talland House, Julia pursued her philanthropy and her nursing. One of Virginia's earliest memories was the look on her mother's face as she came back into the garden after visiting a man called Phillips who had just died after being crushed on the railway line. Leslie, too, recalls this incident and he includes in his *Mausoleum Book* notes from a friend of his sister's, Mrs Grier, to whom they loaned Talland House the winter after Julia's death. Mrs Grier records conversations with many of the townspeople who remembered Julia's help and care for them and their families. According to Mrs Grier's accounts, relayed to Leslie, Julia already had the status of a saint among the poor of St Ives:

"Ah, Ma'am", she said with a beaming face, "when she heard my poor lad was ill, she came at once to see what she could do. She stayed with me and helped me to nurse him herself and got a trained nurse for him; and when she saw him lying dead, she cried over me and kissed me and comforted me, and she gave me this mantle to make me look more respectable."[16]

This view is confirmed by Dr Nicholls in a letter to George Duckworth after Julia's death, when he notes the gratitude expressed for Julia's help in scores of the homes he visited on his rounds.[17]

Virginia records finding her mother's closed writing-desk which had been brought back to London with just one day's worth of letters, from family but also strangers, for her to deal with. These included begging letters, requests for help with family problems, unhappy love affairs, or unemployment: 'Each evening she sat at her table, after some laborious afternoon, her hand moving ceaselessly, at the last a little erratically, as she wrote answers, advice, jests, warning, sympathy, her wise brow and deep eyes presiding, so beautiful still, but now so worn, so profoundly experienced that you could hardly call them sad.'[18]

Julia at her desk in the drawing room at Talland House, 1892

Virginia, however, loses patience with what she came to see as her mother's self-inflicted 'martyrdom'. She felt neglected in favour of the sick, the troubled and the poor. She claimed that a nurse could have looked after Leslie better when he was ill and a governess taught the children more effectively and accurately than the often-impatient Julia. In Virginia's opinion, Julia did not need to take everything onto herself. Julia was in fact a very practised and practical nurse. Her manual, *Notes for Sick Rooms*, had been published in 1883. Despite her disclaimer in the Preface suggesting her lack of experience, this contains very detailed and practical advice on how to care for the sick, based on years of first-hand experience. It ranges from the importance of removing crumbs from the bedclothes, how to make a linseed poultice or remove excess grease from beef tea, to how to deal with visitors or how to lay out a body should the patient die. Like Mrs Ramsay, she was appalled at the insanitary conditions of the St Ives cottages and the lack of medical care available for the poor. 'No hospital on the whole island. It was a disgrace. . . . A model dairy and a hospital up here – those two things she would have liked to do, herself. But how?'[19] Virginia, clearly mimicking over-heard adult conversations, recorded:

Mrs Stephen who is really like a 'Good Angel' to the poor of St Ives is now trying to get enough 'Filthy Lucre' to start a nurse in the town. In her pilgramages [sic] among the poor she has discovered the real want of one and with Mrs Hain Mrs Staff and a few other ladies she has already made a start. This is not a new scheme of Mrs Stephen's but it seems that few other ladies have had the courage or wits to start a similar adventure. We heartily wish the plan all the success it deserves.[20]

The scheme was a success, as evidenced by a public notice in the *St Ives Times and Echo* for September 2nd, 1893:

ST IVES NURSING ASSOCIATION
A trained nurse has been engaged, under the direction of a committee of ladies to attend upon the SICK POOR of St Ives, free of cost and irrespective of creed. Donations or annual subscriptions are earnestly requested, also gifts of old linen, which may be sent to Mrs E HAIN, Jun., Treloyhan, St Ives or Mrs LESLIE STEPHEN, Talland House, St Ives. (22, Hyde Park Gate, London). Mrs

HUGHES, of Tregenna Castle Hotel, has also kindly consented to receive subscriptions. [21]

In spite of appeals by Leslie and others to reduce her workload, Julia 'sank, like an exhausted swimmer, deeper and deeper in the water.'[22]

Her obituary in the *St Ives Times* records:

Mrs Stephen . . . was well known at St Ives, where she was much beloved and respected. With her talented husband and children the deceased lady used to spend a portion of each summer at their St Ives residence (Talland House), and her genial and happy disposition endeared her to rich and poor alike. Mrs Stephen was a prominent member of the St Ives Nursing Association, in which she took great personal interest, and she will be much missed in the Borough. Great sympathy is expressed on all hands with Mr Leslie Stephen and his family in their bereavement.[23]

After her death Julia's work for the sick of St Ives became her legacy and memorial there. The Julia Prinsep Stephen Nursing Association was formally set up in 1896. This was largely due to Stella and to friends such as Mrs Hain. Leslie Stephen contributed £200, the Hain family £300, and other donations came from George Meredith, and the Stillman and Symonds families among others. In 1920 Albany House, next door to Talland House, was converted into a cottage hospital funded by Sir Edward Hain as a memorial to his son who was killed at Gallipoli. This hospital was handed over to the Nursing Association. Stella was on the committee and after her death Vanessa took her place. The Edward Hain Hospital is still a valued local amenity in St Ives.

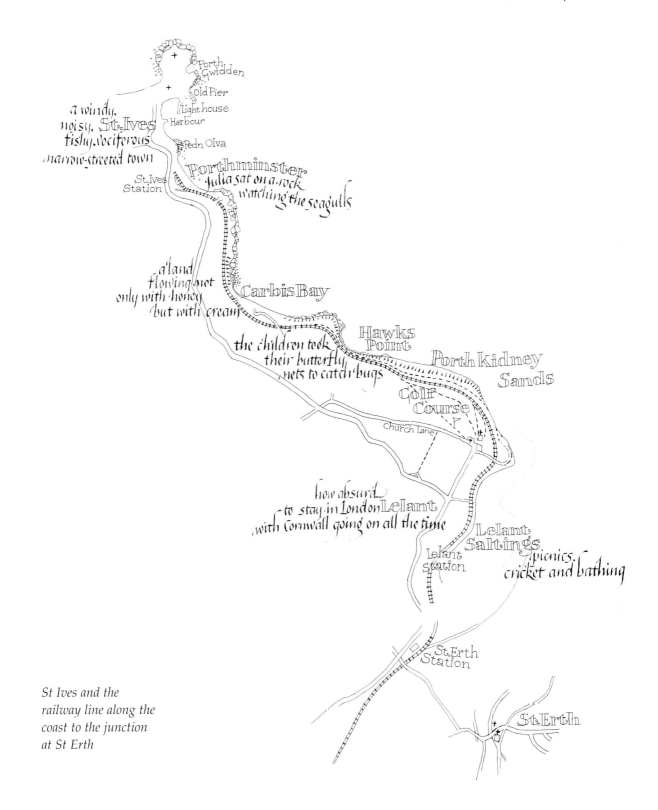

Porth Gwidden

Old Pier

Lighthouse

Harbour

a windy, noisy, St. Ives fishy, vociferous narrow-streeted town

Pedn Olva

Porthminster

Julia sat on a rock watching the seagulls

St. Ives Station

a 'land flowing not only with honey but with cream

Carbis Bay

the children took their butterfly nets to catch bugs

Hawks Point

Porth Kidney Sands

Golf Course

Church Lane

how absurd to stay in London on Lelant with Cornwall going on all the time

Lelant Saltings picnics, cricket and bathing

Lelant Station

St. Erth Station

St. Erth

St Ives and the railway line along the coast to the junction at St Erth

Virginia Woolf

There were then days of pure enjoyment – I conceive them at St Ives most readily.

Virginia Woolf [1]

Virginia remembered childhood summers at Talland House as the happiest time of her life. Her nephew, Quentin Bell, claimed that although she later loved many other places 'for Cornish people and Cornish things she had a kind of patriotic emotion'.[2] St Ives was not just a place of happy childhood memories but also a place of profound spiritual and creative significance for her. More than fifty years later she wrote of what she called her most important memory:

If life has a base that it stands upon, if it is a bowl that one fills and fills and fills – then my bowl without a doubt stands upon this memory. It is of lying half asleep, half awake, in bed in the nursery at St Ives. It is of hearing the waves breaking, one, two, one, two, and sending a splash of water over the beach; and then breaking one, two, one, two, behind a yellow blind. It is of hearing the blind draw its little acorn across the floor as the wind blew the blind out. It is of lying and hearing this splash and seeing this light, and feeling, it is almost impossible that I should be here; of feeling the purest ecstasy I can conceive.[3]

Virginia was first taken to Talland House in 1882 when she was only a few months old and spent the first thirteen summers of her life there. Like her brothers and sisters, she relished the freedom of St Ives after their winters in London. She loved playing in the garden, especially cricket. She loved playing on the beach, paddling, swimming, poking in rock pools, picnicking, boating and fishing. As she got older she loved walking and visiting the town of St Ives and the stunning countryside around it.

Favourite Walks

A favourite walk led by Leslie Stephen was up Trencrom, just outside St Ives, from the top of which one can see St Michael's Mount on the south coast, in one direction, and the Godrevy Lighthouse on the north, in the other.

They nicknamed it Trick Robin and climbed onto the Logan Rock where, as Virginia remembered, 'the hollow in the rough lichened surface was for the victim's blood. . . . Little paths led up to the hill, between heather and ling; and our knees were pricked by the gorse . . . with its sweet nutty smell.'[4] They often walked, collecting moths and botanical specimens, in the nearby woods, one of which they named Fairyland, or squelched through the Halsetown bog where osmunda grew.

The view from Trencrom with the Godrevy lighthouse (just visible)

While Virginia first loved these walks on which her mother encouraged the children to go, she later came to resent them. 'Father must have one of us to go out with him, Mother insisted. Too much obsessed with his health, with his pleasures, she was too willing, as I think now, to sacrifice us to him.'[5] Virginia's complex feeling for her parents is in part worked out through the fictionalisation of them as Mr and Mrs Ramsay, in *To the Lighthouse*. She claimed this to have been cathartic, freeing her especially from what she later came to see as an obsessive relationship with her mother. Her feelings for her father, too, changed as she got older and her essay about him written in 1932, and published in *The Captain's Death Bed and Other Essays*, is much less angry.

The Sea and the Lighthouse

It was the location of Talland House rather than the house itself which made it so appealing to her. From its windows and its garden surrounded by its escallonia hedge the children could clearly see the Godrevy Lighthouse, and this Virginia immortalised in *To the Lighthouse*.

Godrevy Lighthouse 1890

The boat trip which later became the novel's genesis is well known and recorded in the *Hyde Park Gate News* of September 12th, 1892:

On Saturday morning Master Hilary Hunt and Master Basil Smith came up to Talland House and asked Master Thoby and Miss Virginia Stephen to accompany them to the light-house as Freeman the boatman said that there was a perfect tide and wind for going there. Master Adrian Stephen was much disappointed at not being able to go.[6]

Virginia, however, did reach the Lighthouse on that occasion and was not even sea-sick as was Master Basil Smith who 'spued like fury' on the way home. Virginia loved being by the sea throughout her life. Boat trips were one of her favourite activities. In her newspaper for Monday October 3rd, 1892 she records:

On Monday Mr Stephen with his youngest son and daughter went down to the pier and there looked about for a boat. After a long time of waiting a man appeared. They were soon out and sailing merrily along. There was a good breeze and it not being too calm the party was in high spirits. "The music of the water" as Mr Mitchel says beating against the boat the gulls puffins and other sea birds making so harmonious a sound that it would delight the ears of a musician. The sail ended happily by seeing the sea pig or porpoise.[7]

Another expedition is recorded on August Monday 29th, 1892, revealing childish glee at an adult's discomfort:

Mrs Hunt kindly invited the juveniles to go out fishing on Thursday morning at 7 A.M. with her son. The proposal was unanimously appreciated and punc-

tually at 7 o'clock did the juveniles appear. Miss Street who had never seen the Ocean before and had much less been on it was to be one of the party and many guesses were currant as to how she would undergo the trials awaiting her. At about a quarter past seven she stepped into the boat with a calm face but in ten minuits she showed some of the expected signs and leaned over the boat as if in rediness for her fate. She looked pale and showed all the usual signs of sea-sickness. The giggling juveniles looked on at the first part of the scene but turned away from the second as Miss Street disgorged her contents much too liberally for the spectators. The rest of the party did not suffer in the same way but Mr Hilary Hunt said that it made a chap feel spewish to see her. On account of Miss Street the fishers returned home quickly the only thing caught was a gurnard the catcher being Mr Thoby Stephen.[8]

Back in London Virginia had a toy Cornish lugger, which she used to sail on the Round Pond in Kensington Gardens. One tragic day this boat was sunk but was later recovered by a man dredging up weeds and returned to its grateful owner. Her mother made new sails for it and her father renewed the rigging. It was just such a lugger, with the Godrevy Lighthouse in the background, that Vanessa painted on tiles for the fireplace in Virginia's bedroom at Monk's House some forty years later.

Virginia was taken to St Ives each summer for thirteen years; a happy period which came to an abrupt end with the death of her mother, Julia, in May 1895 and the subsequent selling of Talland House later that year. The loss of her mother and of Talland House was ever inextricably linked in her consciousness and both caused a huge caesura.

Writing and St Ives

Her time in St Ives then was hugely formative in Virginia Woolf's personality and in her apprenticeship as a writer. From the first her experience of St Ives and her creative development were linked. In 1905 she wrote to tell Violet Dickinson that she was planning a major work on the 'nature and characteristics of the county of Cornwall' playfully adding that this and another work in progress, showed great promise – 'because they are still unwritten.'[9] In fact, Virginia began using St Ives and Cornwall as her setting and inspiration long before this, as soon as she could make up stories and write, and went on to do so for the rest of her life. All four Stephen children used to write family newspapers together, but the prime mover and most productive writer was always Virginia.

Hyde Park Gate News

Her long-lasting journal was the *Hyde Park Gate News* and competitors were discouraged. The edition for Monday June 27th, 1892 reports: 'We hear that Master Adrian Stephen has commanded a journal whose appellation is "The Talland House Gazette". The author and editor (those two functions being fulfilled by Master Adrian Stephen) has been strongly advised to give up writing by himself but to join with this respectable journal. We have not yet had time to look over "The Talland Gazette" with a view to criticism. We hope that Master Adrian Stephen will take the advice of his parent and give up "The Talland Gazette" altogether.'[10] It appears that he soon did so.

In these papers the daily life of the Stephen family was chronicled and many entries relate to their time in Cornwall, which obviously provided plenty of copy for a young journalist. Her accounts of family life are lively and appealing. The language is precocious and not always entirely accurate, reflecting the maturity of her reading matter and discussions with her father. The perspective though is naive, that of the child who often reveals to an adult reader more than she actually says. The edition of July 18th, 1892, details an expedition to a farm near Trencrom on which the Stephen children were invited by Dr Nicholls. To their dismay he had also invited Mrs Olsson. While the adults disappeared inside 'the juveniles meanwhile employed themselves in making a hole into which they jumped'.[11] They all enjoyed a farmhouse tea of bread, jam and cream.

The *Hyde Park Gate News* came out regularly each Monday and

Virginia waited anxiously for her parents' response and approval. There were items of family news and gossip, arrivals and departures of friends and relations, accounts of Stella's photography, presents they gave and received, and exploits of Shag their well-loved dog. In her newspaper, and later in her memoirs, there are evocative descriptions full of local colour but with her own original perspective and gloss, of the Regatta, the fishing, the swimming and local people and events. In the edition of September 12th, 1892 is an account of Thoby's birthday party which gives a wonderful sense of a large, happy, extended family on holiday.

Facsimile of an extract from the Hyde Park Gate News, *September 12th 1892, describing Thoby's birthday party*

Facsimile of a page from Hyde Park Gate News, *Christmas 1891, with Virginia's serial story set in St Ives*

There is a sense that this is just one of many such occasions showing that Stephen family life, at least at St Ives, was much freer, noisier, more relaxed and happy than many biographers portray it. Indeed, Virginia herself worried that she might have contributed to the mistaken impression that the 'family was one of insane gloom.'[12] There are many accounts of the older Duckworths, and their friends such as Madge Vaughan, Lisa Stillman, Jack Hills, Walter Headlam and Margaret Lushington, all playing with the younger Stephen children. They taught them cricket, and how to hunt bugs and catch moths, they made them butterfly nets and took them on walks. One can see how devastating it was for Vanessa and Virginia when all this came to an end.

There was usually an episode of a serial story in each edition of the *Hyde Park Gate News*. One of Virginia's earliest, written when she was only ten, was set in St Ives.

The Stephen children often made up stories while they walked, a practice Virginia continued throughout her life, and even back in London winters they composed tales located in the Talland House garden. One such serial was about Beccage and Hollywinks, 'spirits of evil who lived on the rubbish heap; and disappeared through a hole in the escallonia hedge.'[13] She told this story to her mother and her godfather, James Lowell, and it resurfaces in her fiction.

History of St Ives

In the *Hyde Park Gate News* and later, more reflectively, in her memoirs, Virginia also wrote detailed, graphic, social histories of the town at the end of the nineteenth century. She shows an awareness of its history and especially of the fishing industry on which its precarious prosperity was based.

Both at the time, first hand, and later from memory, she wrote about the town, the Regatta, the swimming races, and the fishing. She remembered the time before many tourists came:

In those days St Ives, save for ourselves and casual wandering painters, had no summer visitors. Its customs were its own customs; its festivals its own too. There was the August Regatta. Then once in every twelve years or so, old men and women over seventy danced around Knills Monument – a granite steeple in a clearing –and the couple who danced the longest was given a shilling? half a crown? – by the Mayor - Dr Nicholls, on that occasion, who wore a long fur

St Ives mackerel fleet going out to sea, c.1890

trimmed cloak. St Ives had a relic, but a relic in use, of the past - Charlie Pearce, the town crier. Now and again he shuffled along the front swinging a muffin bell and crying "Oyez, Oyez, Oyez." What he went on to say, I do not know, save that on one occasion, when a visitor at Talland House lost a brooch, she had it cried by Charlie Pearce.[14]

Like much of Virginia's writing, it slips between fact and fiction so that many characters and incidents re-emerge in other contexts. The incident of the lost brooch, for instance, figures in *To the Lighthouse.* As when most of us recollect events over twenty, thirty or more years, there are also many instances where she misremembers facts. She acknowledges this by her tentative question marks. The town crier at this time was Charley Paynter, not Charlie Pearce, and the details of the rituals at Knills Steeple are wrong. Her memories of St Ives are inevitably subjective but none the less valuable for that, though they do need to be treated with caution if read as factual social history.

A lugger coming into the harbour at St Ives, c.1900

Memories

Not all that Virginia remembered about Talland House was pleasant. Two confused memories were connected with the mirror in the hallway just outside the dining room door. When only six or seven years old she could only just reach up to see in the mirror but she would never look at herself if anyone else were there. In spite of the celebrated ethereal beauty which she, Stella and Vanessa had inherited from their mother, Virginia never felt confident about her own appearance She rarely looks into a camera lens, but always turns uncomfortably away. She felt what she called 'a looking-glass shame'[15], possibly, she thought, because of some puritan streak inherited from the Stephen family. She often told the story of her grandfather, James Stephen, who renounced cigars for life because he once enjoyed smoking one. Virginia's feelings of guilt and unease are possibly linked with the other unpleasant memory of an incident at Talland House. She remembered her step-brother, Gerald Duckworth, lifting her onto the serving shelf under the mirror in the hall and running his hands over her body under her dress. She had nightmares throughout her life about looking into a mirror and seeing a horrific animal face peering over her shoulder in her reflection. It is another image which finds its way into her fiction, especially in her short story 'The Lady in the Looking Glass: A Reflection'.

Moments of Being

Most of her memories, however, were happy. It was here that she experienced what she later called 'moments of being', apparently insignificant events which came to have a highly charged importance, both for her as a person and as a writer. Almost at the end of her life she articulated her theory that only certain events are remembered and most of life is lived in a state of what she called 'non-being', which she likened to cotton-wool padding surrounding those moments of heightened consciousness. For her, it was not the event itself which was significant but her emotional response to it. She agonised over how to represent in fiction how a day is lived. In her memoir she gives examples from her own life of three such numinous moments and all are located in the garden of Talland House in her childhood. Their potency had lasted some fifty years. She remembers fighting with Thoby on the lawn at Talland House and then a sudden feeling of revulsion at the idea of hurting anyone, which led her suddenly to walk away from the 'pommelling' and to experience a profound feeling of sadness and loneliness. Another memory is of overhearing her parents discussing the suicide of a friend of theirs, Mr Valpy. 'The next thing I remember is being in the garden at night and walking on the path by the apple tree. It seemed to me that the apple tree was connected with the horror of Mr Valpy's suicide. I could not pass it. I stood there looking at the grey-green creases of the bark – it was a moonlit night - in a trance of horror. I seemed to be dragged down, hopelessly, into some pit of absolute despair from which I could not escape. My body seemed paralysed.'[16] The third memory is of seeing a flowerbed by the front door. '"That is the whole", I said. I was looking at a plant with a spread of leaves; and it seemed suddenly plain that the flower itself was a part of the earth; that a ring enclosed what was the flower; and that was the real flower; part earth; part flower.'[17]

In her memoir she reflects on these epiphanies and her responses to them, and realises that it is the shock of such experiences, the desire to probe and explain them, to make connections, which has made her a writer. 'I make it real by putting it into words. It is only by putting it into words that I make it whole; this wholeness means that it has lost its power to hurt me; it gives me, perhaps because by doing so I take away the pain, a great delight to put the severed parts together. 'Painstakingly she perfects her philosophy that behind the cotton wool is hidden a pattern; that we – I mean all human beings – are connected with this; that the whole world is a work of art; that we are parts of the work of art. . . . This intuition of mine – it is so instinctive that it seems given to me, not made by me – has certainly given its scale to my life ever since I saw the flower in the bed by the front door at St Ives.'[18]

Virginia's writing became more experimental and impressionistic. She articulates in 'A Sketch of the Past', written in April 1939, the power of her memories of St Ives and their sensual, impressionist nature, paradoxically both tangible yet evanescent:

Sound and sight seem to make equal parts of these first impressions. When I think of the early morning in bed I also hear the caw of rooks falling from a great height. The sound seems to fall through an elastic, gummy air; which holds it up; which prevents it from being sharp and distinct. The quality of the air above Talland House seemed to suspend sound, to let it sink down slowly, as if it were caught in a blue gummy veil. The rooks cawing is part of the waves breaking – one, two, one, two – and the splash as the wave drew back and then it gathered again, and I lay there half awake, half asleep, drawing in such ecstasy as I cannot describe.[19]

The rhythms and tropes of the sea ebb and flow through Virginia's writing as does the quality of light and colour associated with St Ives. While Vanessa used canvas and brushes, Virginia created increasingly sensual and impressionist word paintings. One of the most beautiful is of her mother at Talland House:

My mother would come out onto her balcony in a white dressing gown. There were passion flowers growing on the wall; they were great starry blossoms, with purple streaks, and large green buds, part empty, part full. If I were a painter I should paint these first impressions in pale yellow, silver, and green. There was the pale yellow blind; the green sea; and the silver of the passion flowers. I should make a picture that was globular; semi-transparent. I should make a picture of curved petals; of shells; of things that were semi-transparent; I should make curved shapes, showing the light through, but not giving a clear outline.[20]

Childhood's End

Julia Stephen died on May 5th, 1895 and that year for the first time Virginia did not spend her summer in St Ives but instead at Freshwater on the Isle of Wight. Topographically it resembles Cornwall with its high cliffs, pounding seas and moorland with gorse and heather. There is even a lighthouse. It was the home of Julia Margaret Cameron, Virginia's great aunt, and had many family connections. But Virginia was to return to St Ives seeking solace, renewal and inspiration, for the rest of her life, for the final time in 1936.

Going Back

Leslie Stephen would no longer return to Cornwall. His death, however, on February 22nd, 1904, released his children from his many restrictions. Their first liberation was to travel to Manorbier on the Pembroke Coast, again drawn by the sea, then more daringly to Italy and to Paris. Their second liberation was from the confinements of Hyde Park Gate to their new home at 46 Gordon Square, Bloomsbury. Thirdly, they decided to return together to St Ives which they did, arriving in August 1905. They stayed at a guest house called Trevose View in Carbis Bay, a village just a short walk round the headland from St Ives and only one stop away on the train. The house had wonderful sea views and Virginia noted all the different ships going up and down the channel and the lack of inhibitions among the holidaymakers on the beach, which appealed to her sense of humour:

We seem to have come to a common agreement here not to look surprised at bare heads & hands; to accept hair flying in the wind, & bathing towels wrapped round the neck, as the simple & natural things. This unconventionality of dress is reflected in the tanned faces & the free stride of the legs. . . . The results are sometimes a little crude, perhaps; ladies, stout & middle aged, conceive themselves under this fresh stimulant in their first youth again; shorten their skirts, throw aside their bonnets, & caper as they walk.[21]

Virginia thought she was living 'among the fields of paradise, among gods', surrounded by moors and hills and a land 'flowing not only with honey but with cream.'[22]

Carbis Bay with bathing machines, c.1900

On their first evening they crept up to Talland House and peeped at it from behind the escallonia hedge. Comfortingly, but also uncannily, nothing appeared to be changed:

There was the house, with its two lighted windows; there on the terrace were the stone urns, against the bank of tall flowers; all, so far as we could see was as though we had but left it in the morning. But yet, as we knew well, we could go no further; if we advanced the spell was broken. . . . We hung there like ghosts in the shade of the hedge, & at the sound of footsteps we turned away.[23]

Probably it felt that, while shatteringly traumatic changes had been going on in their London lives, time had magically been suspended in St Ives. Virginia felt as if she were held by a spell, enchanted. It seemed 'a strange dream . . . a ghostly thing to do.'[24] Perhaps, though, they simply

Opposite: An article by Leonard Woolf in the St Ives Times and Echo, *May 1st 1964*

enjoyed the frisson of visiting their old home in secrecy and darkness, for such deviousness was in fact unnecessary. They were invited to go openly to the house and to have tea with the new owners, Thomas Millie Dow and his family. They found them 'a delightful pair of artists with a family of the age we used to be.'[25] Still, they felt 'like disembodied ghosts' as they wandered round the town, finding it little changed, though a wide road had replaced the rough path and there were many more large mansions. Many people remembered them and their parents. They were able to walk up to Trencrom, as they had done each Sunday with their father, and see again the magnificent view; one way to St Michael's Mount and the other to the Godrevy Lighthouse. Virginia realised with surprise that now she was so much taller, the view was so much wider and far-reaching than she remembered it. Even the dunghill at Peacock Farm, just below Trencrom, was still there.

They had what Virginia called 'a life of pastoral simplicity.'[26] She wrote and Vanessa painted; Thoby and Adrian discussed law and played piquet. They all played cards – Racing Demon and Bridge. In the afternoons they walked and visited old haunts further afield, Land's End, Castle-an-Dinas, St Buryan and Gurnard's Head among them. Always Virginia recorded what she saw and her response to it: 'Lovely are these autumn days on the heath; the gorse is still as smooth as silk, & the air fragrant. I had almost said, regretful, as though there were some tinge of melancholy in its sweetness. All the months are crude experiments out of which the perfect September is made.'[27]

Virginia often also walked on her own, often for great distances, when

Moors and head-lands near the Land's End

she reflected on the landscape, the state of Cornish roads, and the lives of the people around her. She stopped at farms, talked to people, looked at their homes and their occupations, listened to their conversations and rhythms of speech. All was stored away for future writing.

They went boating and fishing and again saw the Regatta. These events obviously remained vivid in Virginia's memory for she later told them to Leonard Woolf who, long after her death, wrote about them in an article for the *St Ives Times and Echo* for May 1st, 1964.

The four discussed plans to rent a farm in the area, which they estimated would cost them £10 a year, a realistic sum at the time, and a project which Virginia continued to pursue on and off throughout her life.

In her letter to Violet Dickinson of August 27th, 1905, Virginia complains of nothing happening and no visitors to their Carbis Bay guest house, but by October 1st she lists the many visitors they had had in the previous four weeks, showing how many other people

---

VIRGINIA WOOLF AT ST. IVES

IT is not well known that Talland House, St. Ives, was the childhood home of the novelist Virginia Woolf, who died in 1941. Her husband, Leonard Woolf, himself a distinguished writer, has sent us this evocative memoir. Mr. Woolf now lives in Lewes, Sussex.

VIRGINIA WOOLF was the daughter of Sir Leslie Stephen and the scene of her novel, "To the Lighthouse," though ostensibly in Scotland, is really St. Ives, and the lighthouse is the one whose light she used to see when as a child she spent the summer in Talland House. Her father bought the lease of Talland House in 1881 and all through her childhood the whole family year after year used to spend the summer in St. Ives. She and her two brothers and her sister loved the house, the town, and indeed the whole of Cornwall. Her father was a great mountaineer and a tremendous walker and, as the children grew up, he took them for his long walks far and wide over the country between St. Ives and Penzance and Land's End. Her mother was a woman of great beauty and charm and, like many Victorian ladies, she was devoted to what was called "good works." She became very well-known and apparently beloved by many of the people living in St. Ives.

THE RETURN

All this came to an end in 1895 and Talland House was sold or rather, I suppose, the lease was given up, for I do not think that the Stephen family ever owned the freehold. For ten years none of the family visited St. Ives, but in August, 1905 Virginia Woolf, with her brother and sister, spent several weeks there. She kept a diary which shows how well the family was remembered and how fond they were of everything connected with the town. The moment they arrived in the late evening they went up to Talland House and "peered through a chink in the escallonia hedge." "There," she writes, "was the house, with its two lighted windows; there on the terrace were the stone urns, against the bank of tall flowers; all, so far as we could see, was as though we had but left it in the morning; but yet, as we knew well, we could go no further; if we advanced the spell was broken."

WALK TO TRENCROM

Next day they walked to Trencrom, which ten years before had been their usual Sunday walk, and found that very little had changed, not even the large dunghill at Peacock Farm. They hired a fishing boat and sailed in the bay and came on a school of porpoises. In the evening they were surprised to see the seine boats rowing out beyond the point, for in those days the pilchards rarely appeared before October. However, they strolled up from the hotel to the little white house on the crest of the hill where the huer sat watching the movements of the "floating cloud of pilchards." They joined a little crowd of Cornish fisherfolk clustered round the huers' seats and listened to them talking about "tucking" and "shooting the seine."

One day they went into the church, and the caretaker, an eld-

erly woman in black, began to talk to them. Suddenly she stopped and asked them whether they had ever had friends in St. Ives, and when they told her that they had themselves lived there every summer for 13 years, she cried, "Ah, you are Mr. Stephen—let me shake you by the hand, my dear. Sit down a moment and talk to me." They sat down and talked to her for half an hour; she had heard a rumour that they had come back and were staying in the town, and she poured out her memories of their mother. Owing to this meeting, they set aside one day "as a day of pilgrimage to certain old St. Ives people, who in spite of the passage of eleven years, still cherish some faithful memory of us." They called on Jinny Berriman, who kept an eating shop, and Mrs. Daniels who was married to a carpenter and had done their washing. They went to see Mr. and Mrs. Pasco, who lived "in one of those delightful cottages beneath the apple trees on the steep hill leading from the beach." Everywhere they were met with affection and a torrent of reminiscences.

PILCHARDS IN THE BAY

One day there was the St. Ives regatta and this carried them right back to the days of their childhood. And then a day or two before they had to return to London, at 9 in the morning they suddenly heard a cry of "Pilchards in the bay." They went up to the huer's house on the point where there was a crowd of watchers, some with megaphones and others with globes tied up in white bags. "The schools of fish were still passing through the bay and all the pilchard boats were in motion like long black insects with rows of legs." The following account of what happened is perhaps worth quoting from the diary:

"The crowd was now gathering and we walked from one point to another vainly trying to interpret the hoarse commands of the megaphones which might, for all we understood of them, have been in Cornish. Mr. Hain came running down again after a time with the word that another school was sighted round the headland .... The school having rounded the point was the property apparently of the Carbis Bay boats, which had hitherto remained at anchor. They were now under way, and the huer who directed them had clambered on to the roof of the huer's house to make his directions more forcible. The boats came slowly towards the floating shadow which we thought we could detect beyond the Carrack rocks. As they neared it the megaphones roared like foghorns. A certain dwarf in particular had leapt to the roof and was brandishing the white globes as though they were dumb-bells. The boats began to drop the seine; they had half completed the circle when a storm of abuse broke from the Huer's house. Language such as

I will not try to reproduce swore at them for a boatload of incompetent monkeys; the school was further to the west and not a fish would enter the nets. 'To the west, west, west,' roared the megaphones .... The Huers could actually see the fish slipping past the point and the net cast in empty water .... The net finally enclosed a small portion of the school and the rest fell a prey to rival boats. Four seines were now shot and we thought it time to take a boat to the first of them .... We .... were rowed out to the spot .... We took up our paces by the row of corks and waited; after a time the empty pilchard boats with their baskets drew up and let down a smaller net, called the tucking net, in the centre of the large one, so that all the fish were gathered in a small compass. Now all the boats were a circle round the inner net, and the two boats which held the net gradually drew it up. It was packed with iridescent fish, gleaming silver and purple .... Then the baskets were lowered and the silver was scooped up and flung into the boats ... The fishermen shouted and the fish splashed. The baskets were filled, emptied and plunged into the bubbling mass again, again and again."

Helping the mentally handicapped

A visit to "Martha" on the West Pier next Tuesday between 10 a.m. and 6 p.m. will provide an opportunity to see some of the work now being done for the mentally handicapped of Cornwall at the Curnow centre, Redruth.

"Martha" is the display van owned by Toc H, a Dormobile-type vehicle which has served many good causes, especially in connection with the scheme for helping families with mentally handicapped children in the late holidays.

The van will show a variety of handwork done at the centre and visitors will be invited to help in a practical way by providing raw material for the work, such as pieces of material, patterns and buttons.

The van's visit has been arranged by St. Ives Toc H Women's Association.

were similarly drawn to the St Ives area. Family members Gerald Duckworth and Jack Hills stayed with them; Kitty and Leo Maxse, who had become engaged at Talland House, stayed nearby. Two daughters of friends of their parents came to see them: Imogen Booth, the daughter of Charles Booth, and Sylvia Milman who also studied at the Royal Academy Schools with Vanessa. Then there were Thoby's Cambridge friends, including Saxon Sydney-Turner.

1908

Virginia came again on April 17th, 1908, this time staying at Trevose House, Draycott Terrace, not far from Talland House. She enjoyed her time there, indulging in her favourite occupations of reading, writing and walking in her old haunts. Her beloved Shag was dead but she had Vanessa's dog, Gurth, as companion on her walks. It was cold and windy but Cornwall extended its usual magic over her. 'I observed the singular beauty of leafless but budding trees against a deep blue sea. The sea is a miracle – more congenial to me than any human being.'[28] The man who owned the house was a fisherman, but as the weather often made fishing impossible or mackerel catches were poor, as Virginia records was the case when she was staying there, they rented out rooms to supplement their income. She took her usual interest in the people around her, observing them closely and collecting anecdotes and idio-syncrasies which re-emerge in her fiction. Lodging upstairs there were '"a confidential man" and his wife, and child; and not one of the three has had a bath in the 7 weeks they have been here. So Mrs Rouncefield told me, with a suspicion of pride.'[29] She sends a similar long observation to Lytton Strachey, self-consciously literary, but very revealing of the social history of ordinary St Ives people at the time:

I have a sitting room, which is the dining room, and it has a side-board, with a cruet and silver biscuit box. I write at the dining table, having lifted a corner of the table cloth, and pushed away several small silver pots of flowers. This might be the beginning of a novel by Mr Galsworthy. My landlady, though a woman of 50, has nine children, and once had 11; and the youngest is able to cry all day long.[30]

She is always conscious of crafting what she is seeing, of experimenting and storing it away for future use: 'I sat for an hour (perhaps it was 10 minutes) on a rock this afternoon, and considered how I should describe the colour of the Atlantic. It has strange shivers of purple and green, but if you call them blushes, you introduce unpleasant associations of red flesh.'[31]

While events in St Ives moved slowly, profoundly disturbing changes had taken place in Virginia's life. Adrian joined her at Trevose House on April 23rd but their brother Thoby had died of typhoid fever, contracted in Greece, on November 22nd, 1906. Less than three months later, on February 17th, 1907, her beloved sister, to whom she was so close and on whom she was so emotionally dependent, married Clive Bell. This event Virginia saw, totally unreasonably, in the light of a betrayal and rejection, a breaking of their 'close conspiracy'. Moreover, the Bells now had a baby, Julian, just two months old and their arrival with the nurse on April 24th completely changed things. Virginia's writing was now interrupted by two babies crying. While Virginia and Clive tried to continue their usual artistic or philosophical discussions, Vanessa's attention was constantly distracted by concerns for Julian. Both Clive and Virginia felt excluded by Vanessa's attention for her baby. They took long walks together and indulged, immaturely, in a flirtation, which has been much discussed by biographers. Although the accounts are ambiguous, something obviously happened between them, though it seems improbable that it amounted to anything physical. Virginia clearly feels guilty and realises that Vanessa is the injured party 'though we did not kiss – (I was willing and offered once – but let that be) – I think we "achieved the heights" as you put it'[32] she writes ambiguously. Virginia returned alone to 29 Fitzroy Square on May 2nd and the Bells stayed on.

Christmas 1909

The Stephens were not just summer visitors. In November of the same year, 1908, Virginia and Adrian, with Lytton Strachey, stayed on the Lizard. Virginia stayed there again in March the following year, this time with Clive and Vanessa, though again she left before they did. That Christmas of 1909 she impulsively decided to spend Christmas alone at Lelant. As she explained in a letter to Vanessa, she was walking in Regents Park on the morning of December 24th when she suddenly realised 'how absurd it was to stay in London, with Cornwall going on all the time.'[33] It was then 12.30 but incredibly she managed to catch the one o'clock train from Paddington arriving at 10.30 that evening without 'handkerchief, watch key, notepaper, spectacles,

The Lelant Hotel, now re-named the Badger Inn, c.1915

cheque book, looking glass or coat'. She was the only guest at the Lelant Hotel, now called the Badger Inn, but she appears not to have been lonely or depressed. Rather she was exhilarated, revelling in the unseasonably warm sunny weather, walking on the sands at Lelant and all the way back to her beloved Trencrom. There is a sense of deep contentment in her letters at this time, of enjoying the quiet and her own company. However, the location of the hotel, at the crossroads in the middle of the village, allowed her as always to listen and observe. She could hear carol singing and gossip. She talked to the maid and the landlady 'about the moon and the chickens and the wreck', and to the ferryman about 'trawling, angling and drowned sailors.'[34]

Zennor 1910

Virginia made another hurriedly arranged, brief, visit to the Lelant Hotel only about ten weeks later in early March 1910, this time accompanied by Vanessa and Clive. This was probably to get her out of London to escape the furore in the aftermath of the notorious Dreadnaught Hoax in which she and Adrian had been involved. Virginia however was heading for another breakdown and that spring and early summer she was very ill.

For some of the time she was looked after by Jean Thomas, who ran the nursing home at Twickenham where Virginia had been a patient. As part of her cure and recuperation they took a walking tour in Cornwall in August and September. It was during this time, on August 19th, that Clive and Vanessa's second son, Quentin, was born. Jean Thomas and Virginia stayed at Tintagel and then at the Berrymans' farm, Porthmeor Farm, at Gurnard's Head, near Zennor: 'We walked till 5 in the afternoon, through a perfect September day, along little paths in the turf, looking into deep sea. We tried for tea at this farm house, and were told we could sleep as well. As the one lodging at Zennor was filled 10 times over, virgins sleeping with matrons in one feather bed, we were much relieved.'[35]

There is a great sense of immediacy and of chatting to someone she wishes to interest and amuse, in her letter to Clive. She must have been sitting fancifully watching the sea, aware of the activities of the farm and the idiosyncrasies of her neighbours going on around her:

... it seems likely that two large steamers are going to collide in three minutes. The pigs and geese are making the farmer, a stout man, with a bad leg, hobble across the yard. From what Mrs Berryman says, the great dispute, which parts husband and wife, is whether the geese shall feed on the fields or the moor. . . . It appears that the geese, in taking flight from the tail of the wain, grazed 3 inches of skin off the smallest brats [sic] leg. Mrs B., bringing in jam tarts, and apple pasty, and cream for tea, remarks that one's always in some trouble.[36]

She is also very aware of the history and prehistory of this area of Cornwall where there are numerous stone circles, menhirs, or standing stones, hill forts, burial chambers and Iron Age villages, all surrounded by myth and tales of the supernatural: 'We have been walking among

the most remarkable moors, among barrows, British villages, stone maidens and beehive huts. If it weren't for the excitability of geese at night, this would be the place I should like to live in.'[37]

They walked from Zennor to Lelant and stayed there one night before returning to London.

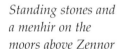

Chysauster Iron Age Village

Standing stones and a menhir on the moors above Zennor

Little Talland House

Virginia and Adrian continued to live in Fitzroy Square but in December that year Virginia took a lease on a weekend house in the village of Firle, near Vanessa's home at Charleston. It is an ugly, unprepossessing villa but it was the first home of her own that Virginia had had. It demonstrates a growing confidence and independence. Ever aware of St Ives, she named it Little Talland House and stained the floors the grey of 'the Atlantic in a storm.'[38]

Mrs Woolf

In 1912 Virginia and Leonard Woolf married. One of the things which they had in common was a love of Cornwall. Leonard Woolf had already been on a number of walking holidays there. In 1901 he was 'on a tramp' with his brother and wrote to Lytton Strachey from their hotel, the King Arthur's Arms Hotel Tintagel: 'The coast is superb – all rocks & I seem to have been balancing on the edge of rocky precipices from all eternity.'39 Like Virginia, however, when he stayed at a small cottage he found his rural idyll disturbed. 'We got no sleep all night – there were fowls roosting just over our heads, a dog howling outside all night, & cows shuffling & kicking in a stall under our room while our beds housed if not as big at least as many animals. But then the sea & the cliffs & the colours make up for everything.'40 In April 1914 Leonard and Virginia enjoyed their first holiday together in St Ives. Virginia had been extremely ill. According to Leonard her mental breakdown lasted from summer 1913 to the autumn of 1915. She had attempted to commit suicide and for some of that time had needed the care of four nurses, two during the day and two at night, as well as Leonard, Vanessa, Janet Case or Ka Cox. Leonard hoped that Cornwall would aid her recovery. He said that her time in Cornwall 'remained in her memory as summer days of immaculate happiness. *To the Lighthouse* is bathed in the light of this happiness and, whenever she returned to Cornwall, she recaptured some of it.'41 Happily this proved to be the case and the three weeks they stayed in various lodgings in St Ives and Carbis Bay, including the Carbis Bay Hotel and a guest house called Godrevy, proved restorative. The weather was good, they went to the races, and rambled over their old haunts. They even 'crept into Talland House itself yesterday, and found it wonderfully done up and spick and span, and all the garden brimming with flowers and rock gardens – very unlike what it was in our day.'42

The Millie Dow family had made great changes, adding an extension at the side, building a coach house and stables, extending the property and renovating the house and grounds.

The Millie Dow family at a refurbished and extended Talland House, c.1912

1916-1919

They went again, with their friend Margaret Llewelyn Davies and her friend Lilian Harris, for a fortnight in September 1916. Their address was Gwel Marten, Carbis Bay. It was earlier that year that D.H. Lawrence and his German wife, Frieda, had decided to come to Cornwall. Like Virginia, he was drawn by the amazing beauty of the place and the sense of wildness and primeval history. They also needed a refuge. They stayed at the Tinners Arms in Zennor, which Lawrence used as a location for his story 'Samson and Delilah', and then moved into one of the three cottages, on which he took a lease at Higher Tregerthen. Another of these, with a tower, he allocated to the writers John Middleton Murry and his wife, Katherine Mansfield, whom he persuaded to join in his experiment in utopian living, which he called Rananim. 'It is a most beautiful place: a tiny granite village nestling under high, shaggy moor-hills, and a big sweep of lovely sea beyond, such lovely sea, lovelier even than the Mediterranean. . . . It is all gorse now, flickering with flower; and then it will be heather; and then, hundreds of foxgloves. It is the best place I have ever been in I think.'[43]

Zennor village and the coast from near Eagle's Nest

Lawrence tended his garden, he and the Murrys wrote and they walked, swam, sunbathed on the rocks and ate together in the evenings. The young local girl, Hilda Jelbert, who cleaned and cooked for them, liked Frieda best, finding her 'jokey, stout and fair'. Lawrence she thought 'moody and sarcastic' and Katherine 'a marvellous-looking woman'[44] who was obviously very ill with a terrible cough. They outraged Hilda by providing beef instead of mutton for her to make Cornish pasties.

Utopia, however, was short lived. Katherine Mansfield loved having the tower for her writing room and was impressed by the beauty of the surroundings but she hated the cold, harsh wind and the damp. Moreover, she could not live with the Lawrences. She felt overpowered by their overt sexuality and verbal and physical aggression towards each other. When she ironically suggested renaming the Lawrences' cottage The Phallus, Frieda agreed! After only five weeks Murry and Katherine left to live on the south coast of Cornwall at Mylor.

The Lawrences stayed on and *Women in Love* was written there, drawing strongly on Mansfield, Murry and incidents from life at Tregerthen, as does the later 'Nightmare' section in *Kangaroo*. However, the real world outside was beginning to impinge. As early as 1916 Lawrence was recording 'the inflated sausage of an airship edging through the blue heavens, and the submarine destroyers nosing like swimming rats up the coast.'[45] Lawrence and Frieda finally had to leave Tregerthen in 1917 because of the suspicions of the local people that they were German spies, signalling to U boats off the coast, events which have been fictionalised by Helen Dunmore in her novel *Zennor in Darkness*.

Virginia and Katherine

Virginia apparently never met the Lawrences in Cornwall. Years later, on hearing news of his death, she recollected to Dorothy Brett that she had never spoken to him but did remember seeing him once 'swinging a spirit lamp in a shop at St Ives.'[46] The Woolfs also knew Murry and Katherine, having met them first at Garsington just before their marriage, but did not meet them in Cornwall, either. Virginia did, though, correspond with Katherine Mansfield, whose work she greatly admired and in 1918 the Woolfs' Hogarth Press published Mansfield's story 'The Prelude'. When Virginia was considering taking over the lease of the Tregerthen cottages from Lawrence, Katherine wrote that

Perhaps the house itself is very imperfect in many ways but there is a – something – which makes one long for it. Immediately you get there – you are free, free as air. You hang up your hat on a nail & the house is furnished – It is a place where you sit on the stairs & watch the lovely light inhabiting the room below. After nightfall the house has three voices – If you are in the tower and someone comes from the far cottage – he comes from far away – You go by the edge of the fields to Katie Berryman's for bread. You walk home along the rim of the Atlantic with the big fresh loaf – & when you arrive the house is like a ship . . . It bewitched me. [47]

Virginia was already bewitched, and possibly in spite of wondering why Katherine had left this idyll so quickly, she could not resist such sales talk. After protracted negotiations and deliberations with the owner, Captain Short, the Woolfs finally took over the lease of the three cottages in 1919 for £5 a year each, but never actually lived there. They instead bought Monk's House, in Sussex.

Eagle's Nest and Zennor

Virginia's friend Ka Cox had married Will Arnold-Forster and, in 1920, instead of sharing the Tregerthen cottages with the Woolfs as Virginia had hopefully planned, they bought Eagle's Nest, a huge house over-looking Tregerthen and the narrow band of farmland along the coast by Zennor. Virginia called it 'too much of a castle-boarding house to be a pleasant object; but considering the winds, firm roots are needed. Endless varieties of nice elderly men to be seen there, come for climb-ing.'[48] There were young men, too, including George Mallory, who later died climbing Everest. His widow Ruth married Will Arnold-Forster after his wife Ka's death. Alison Symons has childhood memories of the Arnold-Forsters when they lived at Eagle's Nest. She then lived at Tremedda, one of the farms on the coastal plain just below. The local people apparently nicknamed Ka Big Stick as she was tall, elegant and forceful. Will was dismissed as Little Stick. Alison's grandmother, Mrs Griggs, used to say that 'he was a painter, politician and gardener, and the only thing he was any good at was gardening!'[49] Ka Arnold-Forster seems to have been well liked in the area and to have thrown herself into local affairs. She was a Justice of the Peace, a Magistrate, a member of the Cornwall County Education Committee and a Governor of St Ives and Penzance Schools. She invited the local children to Eagle's Nest. Alison Symons remembers 'the big treat was to play with her son Mark's clockwork train, which was set out in one of the small gardens. It fascinated us to watch the little trains winding their way around the paths and through tunnels.'[50] During the week Alison Symons lived with her other grandmother, Mrs Florence Millie Dow, at Talland House, so that she could go to school in St Ives.

Eagle's Nest and the three cottages at Tregerthen below

Virginia Woolf seems to have had an ambivalent attitude to the Arnold-Forsters and their life at Eagle's Nest. She indulges in a number of spiteful remarks about them: 'Ka was more like a sack of some of the commoner garden vegetables than ever. . . . Anyhow she tells too many stories about the strange figures who drive up to the Eagle's Nest. Gordon Bottomley, the Ranee of Sarawak.'[51] It is difficult to assess just what the root of this spitefulness was. Ka Cox had been her friend for many years and had nursed her and helped her through many crises. Possibly Virginia was embarrassed that Ka had seen her at her most vulnerable. Virginia admits to envy on hearing about the birth of Ka's son and again on hearing about their purchase of Eagle's Nest, a house she would have liked to be able to afford for herself. Her derogatory comments about Ka are possibly more complex than just envy of her life in Zennor. Ka had been a lively, independent, bohemian. Now Virginia saw her, as she thought, diminished, one of the 'great people of the neighbourhood'[52] a sort of Lady Bountiful who possibly reminded Virginia of Julia and her 'good works' in St Ives. Ka and Julia undoubtedly serve as a composite source for Mrs Durrant in *Jacob's Room*, which Virginia was writing at this time. Mrs Durrant is driven in her carriage out to Zennor to visit Mrs Pascoe in her little cottage and 'advise' her how to cure her potatoes of blight and her leg of its pain.

Poniou 1921

The Woolfs nevertheless continued to accept hospitality from the Arnold-Forsters, though when they went next to Cornwall, in March 1921, they stayed nearby in the hamlet of Poniou. Virginia's excitement is palpable in her diary entry for March 22nd.

Here we are on the verge of going to Cornwall. This time tomorrow – it is now 5.20 – we shall be stepping onto the platform at Penzance, sniffing the air, looking for our trap, & then – Good God! – driving off across the moors to Zennor – Why am I so incredibly & incurably romantic about Cornwall? One's past, I suppose: I see children running in the garden. A spring day. Life so new. People so enchanting. The sound of the sea at night. And now I go back 'bringing my sheaves' – well, Leonard, & almost 40 years of life, all built on that, permeated by that: how much so I could never explain. And in reality it is very beautiful. I shall go down to Treveal & look at the sea – old waves that have been breaking precisely so these thousand years. [53]

They lodged with Mrs Selina Hosking, a widow whose husband, like many Cornish miners, had sought work abroad, and died in the South African mines. Virginia sometimes mistakenly calls her Hosken in her letters and mis-spells the name of the hamlet Ponion, instead of Poniou. They visited the Arnold-Forsters and from their vantage point at Eagle's Nest saw the heather being burned at Tregerthen.

It was on this visit that Virginia wrote one of her most evocative, painterly, descriptions of the area:

By looking over my left shoulder I see gorse yellow against the Atlantic blue, running up, a little ruffled, to the sky, today hazy blue. And we've been lying on the Gurnard's Head, on beds of samphire among grey rocks with buttons of yellow lichen on them. How can I pick out the scene? You look down onto the semi-transparent water – the waves all scrambled into white round the rocks – gulls swaying on bits of seaweed – rocks now dry now drenched with white waterfalls pouring down crevices. No one near us but a coast-guard sitting outside the house. We took a rabbit path round the cliff, & I find myself shakier than I used to be. Still however maintaining without force to my conscience that this is the loveliest place in the world. It is so lonely. Occasionally a very small field is being ploughed, the men steering the plough round the grey granite rocks.[54]

The Gurnard's Head

Christmas 1926

In 1926 the Woolfs spent what seems to have been not a very festive Christmas with the Arnold-Forsters. Virginia complained to Vita Sackville-West of the cold they were enduring there: 'I sleep in stockings, vest, a pair of wool drawers (I had to buy in Penzance) a jacket. The bed gets cold on the right if one sleeps on the left.'[55] Even on Christmas Day she was working, revising drafts for *To the Lighthouse*, and writing in despair to Angus Davidson that all her facts about lighthouses were wrong. She is obviously feeling peevish, calling Will Arnold-Forster 'a water-blooded waspish little man',[56] and deciding to return home a day early.

In early May 1930 the Woolfs were again in Cornwall as part of a book-selling tour through the West Country. Virginia felt her old delight in the landscape as they drove from Penzance to Zennor but a growing sense of nostalgia and loss, 'all the gorse blazing against a pure blue sea, to St Ives; where I saw my Lighthouse, and the gate of my home, through tears – thinking how my mother died at my age; or next year to it.'[57]

Major Writing

All of Woolf's novels are to some extent a reworking of her own past and especially memories of her summers at St Ives. People, places, histories and events that figure in her early newspapers, letters, diaries and later memoirs are also painstakingly crafted into fiction. The light and colour of St Ives illuminate her writing. The sea, granite, fish and moths become potent symbols in her work. Images recur throughout her writing life: rooks rise and sink, the garden gate clicks, the little acorn on the nursery blind trails across the floor, waves rise and fall. The period, roughly 1920 to 1930, was one of draining creativity for Virginia Woolf when she wrote, among many other things, the three novels most closely connected with St Ives: *Jacob's Room* (1922), *To the Lighthouse* (1927) and *The Waves* (1931).

Jacob's Room

She worked seriously on *Jacob's Room* for two years before it was published in 1922. It was the first full-length work published by the Hogarth Press, which Leonard and Virginia had set up in 1917, and Vanessa illustrated its cover. After years of agonising, especially over how to represent character, Woolf came to a quiet confidence: 'I have found out how to begin (at 40) to say something in my own voice.'[58]

The novel is interesting in terms of its relation to Cornwall because its location is undisguised. It names real places and people from around St Ives and clearly draws on memories of the coast around Zennor, the Berrymans' Farm, Poniou and Tregerthen. Jacob Flanders and his friend Timmy Durrant are sailing round the north Cornish coast towards Lands End:

A steamer, probably bound for Cardiff, now crosses the horizon, while near at hand one bell of a fox-glove swings to and fro with a bumble-bee for a clapper. These white Cornish cottages are built on the edge of the cliff; the garden grows gorse more readily than cabbages; and for hedge, some primeval man has piled granite boulders. In one of these, to hold, a historian conjectures, the victim's blood, a basin has been hollowed, but in our times it serves more tamely to seat those tourists who wish for an uninterrupted view of the Gurnard's Head. . . . Two fishing luggers, presumably from St Ives Bay, were now sailing in an opposite direction from the steamer, and the floor of the sea became alternately clear and opaque. As for the bee, having sucked its fill of honey, it visited the teasel and thence made a straight line to Mrs Pascoe's patch, once more directing the tourists' gaze to the old woman's print dress and white apron, for she had come to the door of the cottage and was standing there.[59]

We return to Mrs Pascoe in the final chapter but here we are positioned to see her not from the sea but from the moors behind her cottage:

The Phoenicians slept under their piled grey rocks; the chimneys of the old mines pointed starkly; early moths blurred the heather-bells; cartwheels could be heard grinding on the road far beneath; and the suck and sighing of the waves sounded gently, persistently, for ever. Shading her eyes with her hand Mrs Pascoe stood in her cabbage-garden looking out to sea. Two steamers and a sailing-ship crossed each other; passed each other; and in the bay the gulls kept alighting on a log, rising high, returning again to the log, while some rode in upon the waves and stood on the rim of the water until the moon blanched all to whiteness. Mrs Pascoe had gone indoors long ago.[60]

The rhythmic pounding sound of the sea merges with the sound of guns. The novel is also an elegy for the young men who had died in the First World War, and for Thoby who had died in 1906. The relationship between Betty Flanders and her son, Jacob, can be read as echoing that of Julia and Adrian, or Vanessa and Julian. The powerful opening image of a crab in a bucket, which becomes central to the novel, representing Jacob as crippled and confined, comes straight from days spent playing in rock pools on Porthminster Beach. Other key motifs, which are all factually described in 'A Sketch of the Past', are the death's head moth, bones found on the moors, and the sheep's skull which is taken back to the nursery and hung on the wall. Although there is much realistic detail and specifically named representation of place and people, *Jacob's Room* is in other ways experimental. It is, she claimed, 'a new form for a new novel'.in which she hoped to be able to 'net' her dialogue, a fishing image which she was to use many times to describe her creative method[61]. The novel is full of sense impressions and things in flux, fluctuating. In the opening paragraph, Mrs Flanders is writing a letter:

Slowly welling up from the point of her gold nib, pale blue ink dissolved the full stop; for there her pen stuck; her eyes fixed, and tears slowly filled them. The entire bay quivered; the lighthouse wobbled; and she had the illusion that the mast of Mr Connor's little yacht was bending like a wax candle in the sun. She winked quickly. Accidents were awful things. She winked again. The mast was straight; the waves were regular; the lighthouse was upright; but the blot had spread.[62]

On Saturday morning Master Hilary Hunt and Master Basil Smith came up to Talland House and asked Master Thoby and Miss Virginia Stephen to accompany them to the light-house as Freeman the boatman

said that there was a perfect tide and wind for going there. Master Adrian Stephen was much disappointed at not being allowed to go. On arriving at the light-house Miss Virginia Stephen saw a small and dilapidated bird standing of on one leg on the light-house. Mrs Hunt called the man and asked him how it had got there. He said that it had been blown there and they then saw that it had been blown picked out. On the way home Master Basil Smith "spued like fury".

Facsimile of an extract from the Hyde Park Gate News, *September 12th 1892, describing the boat trip to Godrevy Lighthouse*

To the Lighthouse

It is this Lighthouse at Godrevy of course, which is the central trope in her most famous and fully worked novel about St Ives, *To the Lighthouse*. She intended that her novel would be 'fairly short: to have father's character done complete in it; & mothers; & St Ives; & childhood; & all the usual things I try to put in – life, death &c. But the centre is father's character, sitting in a boat, reciting. We perished each alone, while he crushes a dying mackerel – However I must refrain. I must write a few little stories first, & let the Lighthouse simmer.'[63] As it 'simmered' her project changed and she relocated St Ives fictionally to Skye, though the local detail, events, topography and flora all remain Cornish. There is some debate over why she did this. Since she also removed specific dates and changed names it was possibly to distance her novel from being too overtly autobiographical and give it wider significance. It is a novel about changing perceptions and ambiguities, of the impossibility of pinning anything down, for as James says 'Nothing was ever simply one thing.'[64] She is very clear in her diary and letters, however, that the novel has as its location Talland House and its genesis in events from her Cornish childhood, especially the famous voyage to Godrevy which Adrian had to miss, as she recorded in detail in the *Hyde Park Gate News*.

It is a hugely complex novel in its construction, syntax, imagery and range of meanings, and has been extensively discussed by literary critics and Virginia Woolf's biographers. It is interesting in terms of St Ives because it reworks, in some cases almost word for word, episodes and passages from Virginia's newspapers, letters and diaries relating to what Talland House looked like and their way of life there. There are long passages evocatively describing the garden, the town, the beach and the sea. Lily Briscoe and William Banks walk in the evening:

...for it was bright enough, the grass still a soft deep green, the house starred in its greenery with purple passion flowers, and rooks dropping cool cries from the high blue. But something moved, flashed, turned a silver wing in the air. It was September after all, the middle of September, and past six in the evening. So off they strolled down the garden in the usual direction, past the tennis lawn, past the pampas grass, to that break in the thick hedge, guarded by red-hot pokers like brasiers of clear burning coal, between the blue waters of the bay looking bluer than ever. They came there regularly every evening drawn by some need. It was the way the water floated off and set sailing thoughts which had grown stagnant on dry land, and gave to their bodies even some sort of physical relief. First, the pulse of colour flooded the bay with blue, and the heart expanded with it and the body swam, only the next instant to be checked and chilled by the prickly blackness on the ruffled waves. Then, up behind the great black rock, almost every evening spurted irregularly, so that one had to watch for it and it was a delight when it came, a fountain of white water; and then, while one waited for that, one watched, on the pale semicircular beach, wave after wave shedding again and again smoothly a film of mother-of-pearl.[65]

Virginia has been learning from Vanessa. This is clearly seen through the eyes of a painter who notes colour and changes in colour, light and shade and texture; notes how blue is intensified if placed next to orange; notes form and composition.

Above all there is the lighthouse. Its beam reaches into the house and onto Mrs Ramsay's bed as she is dying. In the final section James, Cam and Mr Ramsay finally reach the lighthouse, sailing in a fishing-boat with Macalister and his boy:

The sails flapped over their heads. The water chuckled and slapped the sides of the boat, which drowsed motionless in the sun. Now and then the sails rippled with a little breeze in them, but the ripple ran over them and ceased. The boat made no motion at all. Mr Ramsay sat in the middle of the boat. He would be impatient in a moment, James thought, and Cam thought, looking at their father, who sat in the middle of the boat between them (James steered; Cam sat alone in the bow) with his legs tightly curled. He hated hanging about. Sure enough, after fidgeting for a second or two, he said something sharp to Macalister's boy, who got out the oars and began to row.[66]

Woolf's writing was becoming more and more impressionist and the meaning more obscure. When Roger Fry asked what the symbolic meaning of the lighthouse might be, she replied, 'I meant *nothing* by The Lighthouse. One has to have a central line down the middle of the book to hold the design together. I saw that all sorts of feelings would accrue to this, but I refused to think them out, and trusted that people would make it the deposit for their own emotions – which they have done, one thinking that it means one thing and another another. I can't manage Symbolism except in this vague generalised way.'[67] Significantly the artist, Lily Briscoe, finally completes her painting, a portrait of Mrs Ramsay sitting on the steps down to the terrace, by drawing a line down the centre. The meaning remains elusive.

The Waves

Her final novel closely based on Cornwall, *The Waves* is even more elusive, metaphysical and impressionist. It begins with a seascape drawn, again with a painterly eye, straight from St Ives: 'The sun had not yet risen. The sea was indistinguishable from the sky, except that the sea was slightly creased as if a cloth had wrinkles in it. Gradually as the sky whitened a dark line lay on the horizon dividing the sea from the sky and the grey cloth became barred with thick strokes moving, one after another, beneath the surface, following each other, pursuing each other, perpetually'[68]

There is no specific naming of location, but Talland House and the sense impressions it held for Virginia, are clearly recognisable:

The light struck upon the trees in the garden, making one leaf transparent and then another. One bird chirped high up; there was a pause; another

chirped lower down. The sun sharpened the walls of the house, and rest-
ed like the tip of a fan upon a white blind and made a blue fingerprint of
shadow under the leaf by the bedroom window. The blind stirred slightly,
but all within was dim and unsubstantial. The birds sang their blank
melody outside.[69]

Friends play cricket in the garden, talk around the table, overhear conversations in the garden. The relationship between mothers and sons is
re-visited. People go walking and boating. Hermione Lee has suggested
that Virginia Woolf is in some ways like a painter such as Monet, who
constantly repeats the same scene, be it a haystack, water lily or Rouen
Cathedral, but in endlessly different ways. In *The Waves*, light, time and
meaning are fluid, indeterminate and even less 'only one thing'. Woolf
likens her memories of St Ives to 'little corks that mark a sunken net.'[70]
In her diary for February 7th, 1931, as she completed *The Waves*, she
expressed the satisfaction that in it she had finally 'netted that fin', her
metaphor for capturing in words the elusive essence of her images
which she has been striving after for all her writing life. 'Thus I hope to
have kept the sound of the sea & the birds, dawn, & garden subcon-
sciously present, doing their work under ground.'[71]

Images from St Ives are not restricted only to her novels and short stories. They surface over and over again in all her writing. In her diary of
January 31st, 1920 she describes her feelings of depression. 'An incident
of this sort is like the blackness that used to cross the waves in the bay
& make my heart sink when I sat doing lessons at the long table in St
Ives drawing room.'[72] Writing in London during the Blitz, she blocked
out unpleasant thoughts by remembering Thoby, 'steering us round the
point without letting the sail flap . . . a schoolboy whose jacket was
rather tight; whose arms shot out of their sleeves . . . I want to go on
thinking about St Ives.'[73] Whether writing fact or fiction she always feels
'a general sense of the poetry of existence that overcomes me. Often it is
connected with the sea & St Ives.'[74]

Endings

Virginia's final visit to the area was in May 1936 when she and Leonard again stayed with the Arnold-Forsters at Eagle's Nest. Virginia was once more close to a nervous breakdown and Leonard hoped that taking her back to Cornwall would be therapeutic. 'As the final cure, we wandered round St Ives and crept into the garden of Talland House and in the dusk Virginia peered through the ground-floor windows to see the ghosts of her childhood.'[75]

The therapy worked, but only for a while.

Ka Cox died in May 1938. Many friends and dignitaries and numbers of local people, including Florence Millie Dow from Talland House, attended her funeral service in Zennor church. Virginia, however, could not make the journey and was never to go to Cornwall again. Her depression had increased and on March 28th, 1941 she committed suicide. Given her lifelong love of the sea it can be no coincidence that the method she chose was to drown herself in the Ouse, where it flows strongly into the nearby ocean. Vita Sackville-West expressed her hope, probably shared by many, that Virginia's body would be swept out to sea, but it was not to be. Leonard Woolf chose an inscription from the end of *The Waves* for her grave in the garden at nearby Monk's House: 'Against you I will fling myself, unvanquished and unyielding, O Death!'[76] The last paragraph of that novel begins, 'And in me too the wave rises. It swells; it arches its back. . . .'[77] The final line is:

The waves broke on the shore.

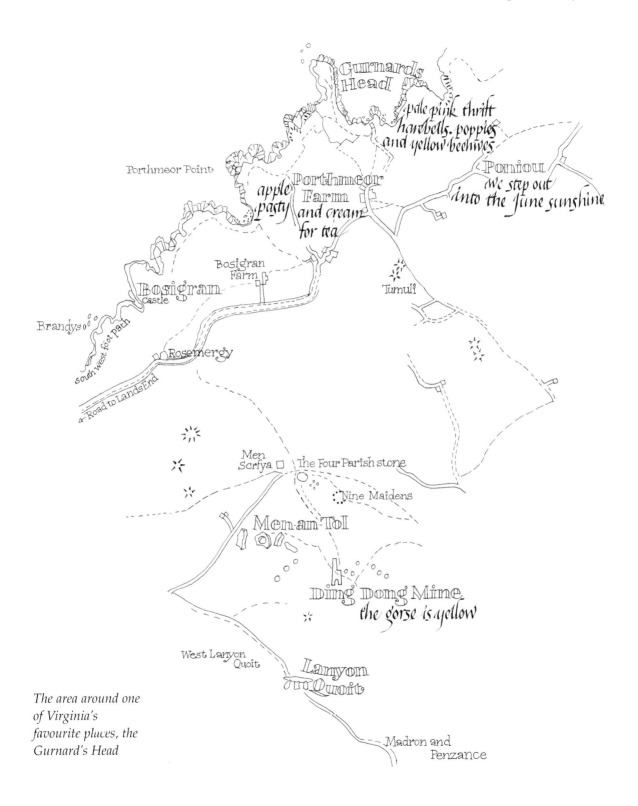

Gurnards
Head

*pale pink thrift
harebells. poppies
and yellow beehives*

Porthmeor Point

Poniou
*we step out
into the June sunshine*

*apple
pasty*
Porthmeor
Farm
*and cream
for tea*

Bosigran
Farm

Tumuli

Bosigran
Castle

Brandys

south west foot path

Rosemergy

↞ Road to Lands End

Men
Scryfa
The Four Parish stone

Nine Maidens

Men-an-Tol

Ding Dong Mine
the gorse is yellow

West Lanyon
Quoit
Lanyon
Quoit

Madron and
Penzance

*The area around one
of Virginia's
favourite places, the
Gurnard's Head*

Vanessa Bell

I cannot remember a time when Virginia did not mean to be a writer, and I a painter.

Vanessa Bell[1]

Vanessa Stephen had an early introduction to Cornwall. She breathed the Cornish air before she could walk and talk. In a letter dated May 18th, 1879 at the imminent birth of his first child by Julia, Leslie Stephen wrote 'I only hope that it [the baby] will be of the right sex i.e. the feminine, as I need hardly say. I like some particular boys; but the genus boy seems to me one of nature's mistakes. Girls improve as they grow up; but the boy generally deteriorates.'[2]

He must therefore have been delighted when Vanessa was born on May 30th, 1879. He went on to say he had a good pair of boys in his stepsons (Gerald and George). Soon after the birth the Stephens planned a holiday trip to Cornwall and Leslie remarked that Vanessa was flourishing.

By September of that year, the family and a nursemaid were spending five weeks at Newquay, where Leslie stated Julia was fully recovered and also that he would be 'quite happy to settle here altogether.' The summer of the following year they spent at Falmouth, which he described as lovely and sleepy, with a clear and brilliantly blue sea. In August 1881 Leslie was enchanted with Fowey: 'We are in a quaint hole at the bottom of a Cornish glen. . . . The children are all rosy and happy; so we regard it as a success. . . .'[3]

By autumn of 1881 Leslie Stephen was back in Cornwall. After many visits to different locations, he had finally found the ideal place. In October he wrote to his friend Charles Eliot Norton that he had bought a house at St Ives:

The children will be able to run straight out of the house to a lovely bit of sand and have good air and quiet. But it makes me feel more than ever that my loco-motive powers are getting terribly hampered. With six children hanging on to my skirts, I have little hope of ever getting farther away than Cornwall, except in imagination.[4]

In 1882 when Vanessa was three, Virginia not yet a year old and Adrian yet to be born, the Stephen family spent their first summer at Talland House. Leslie rejoiced in having made the right decision in buying the lease of the house. They now had a town and a country house. The children, whether in Hyde Park Gate or at Talland House, were never in neglect of their education. Although they had no formal schooling, the Stephen parents were both teachers to their second young family. Stella records 'Mother gave Adrian an hour's lessons.' In the absence of Julia, Leslie wrote to tell her The little ones were very good: all 3 sitting on my knee to look at the bear book & listening whilst Nessa explained with great elocution what you were to do if you met a wild beast in a wood.'[5] The following day he wrote again: 'I had my lunch & saw Nessa do her letters – like a flash of lightning. In fact, she clearly knows them perfectly now, when she chooses, little puss.'[6]

As Vanessa grew older in those long summers of childhood by the sea, her natural eye for colour, shape and form developed. St Ives was a good breeding ground for the talents of a young creative mind. Virginia, at a young age, recognized in her sister a passion for art: 'Once I saw her scrawl on a black door a great maze of lines, with white chalk. "When I am a famous painter - " she began, and then turned shy and rubbed it out in her capable way.'[7] Stella's St Ives diary of 1893 is full of such entries as 'Nessa Mother & I settled down to paint etc. in Rose garden.'- 'Nessa & I sat in garden, she painted I worked.'[8] During those childhood years, she was painting in watercolour and grappling with the difficul-ties of drawing: 'in her spare moments Vanessa read Ruskin's *The Elements of Drawing* and virtuously followed its instructions, filling

small squares with hatching until they looked like grey silk.'[9] The environment began shaping her thoughts and ideas. She was aware of the colony of artists living in the small town: 'that the sea was beautiful and might be painted some day, and perhaps once or twice she looked steadily in the glass when no one was by and saw a face that excited her strangely, her being began to have a definite shape, a place in the world . . .'[10]

Porthminster Hotel with Talland House far right, c.1900

Godrevy Lighthouse

Leslie and Julia Stephen had joined the St Ives Arts Club when it was established in 1890, in a building at Westcotts Quay on the edge of the sea. Although there is no documentary evidence, the children at Talland House might have attended many concerts, plays and parties enjoyed at the Club. They may also have stood at its window, overlooking the harbour and out to Godrevy Lighthouse, whose light Vanessa and Virginia 'saw night by night shine across the bay into the windows of Talland House.'[11] Indeed, whether by night or day, Godrevy lighthouse, standing sentinel on its lonely island just offshore

Opposite: Vanessa at easel, Virginia, Thoby, Adrian

at Gwithian, seemed to be their constant companion. A local boy, Donald Bray, writes of his memories of its beam:

I used to lie in bed watching the beams of Godrevy lighthouse revolving. Their rays would sweep across the ceiling of my bedroom overlooking the Bay. I do remember it as a real comfort, which could send me to sleep . . . whilst last glimpses as I drifted off would be the red flashes of Trevose Head away on the horizon.[12]

Godrevy lighthouse was built in 1859. Its light was described as a bold flashing white beam, and was manned by two keepers. Since 1934 the beam has operated automatically, its light no more than a faint glimmer at ten seconds' intervals, and the small island is now deserted but for the gulls. Extending from the island on which the lighthouse perches is a mile-and-a-half length of reef known as The Stones. These are marked by a black pillar-type buoy with whistle and bell, warning of this dangerous reef, responsible for many shipwrecks. One of the earliest recorded wrecks was 1649, when the *Garland*, bound for France, dragged her anchor while sheltering in St Ives Bay. She was carrying the possessions of the recently executed Charles the First. It is rumoured that gold buttons have at some time been washed ashore. In 1939 St Ives lifeboat lost all its crew to the

Godrevy Lighthouse rocks at Godrevy, save for one man, William Freeman, who had acted as boatman to the Stephens at Talland House.

A Walk into St Ives

Even in so small a town as St Ives, sketch pads and paints were available because of the proliferation of artists. Vanessa and Virginia used to visit Lanham's shop and gallery, where artists displayed their paintings and Whistler had once asked James Lanham 'Why don't you start selling paints. I have to send all the way to Cambridge for my paints.'[13] Virginia remembered they would 'go down to the town and buy penny boxes of tintacks or whatever it might be at Lanham's: Mrs Lanham wore false curls all round her face: the servants said Mr Lanham had married her "from an advertisement".'[14] Stella noted in her diary of 1893: 'M[other] & I went to town saw the pictures. B[ough]t none & odds & ends & met the others returning from sail.' On another visit to the gallery they were 'very much struck by a picture by Mrs Robinson.'[15] And Stella took a photograph of a painting by Mr Robinson.

Laity's shop,
Leonard Fuller

They would have been familiar with Curnows, the bakers in the High Street, who had the largest restaurant in town. They did the catering for many functions and, in an interview with the author, Treve Curnow said

Father was a master baker and confectioner. We used to do the catering for the Arts Club. On President's night we provided a running buffet. The things we made were out of this world, game pies, fish pies, vol-au-vent, various sandwiches and salads, meringues, iced puddings, French and Genoese pastries, Venetian jellies and creams. They really went to town. The cost was one guinea per head.[16]

Charles Simpson sketching on the Wharf

During the thirteen years and long months of childhood in those summer days at Talland House, Vanessa's trips into town would have taken her past the painter Louis Grier's studio on the harbour front, when the sea lapped the net lofts, boat builders, and cottages at its edge, before Wharf Road was built in 1922. The artist's many friends would be capturing sunrise or sunset in paint, the lighthouse on Smeaton's pier, or boats as they sailed out in the bay to the fishing grounds. Louis Grier was a favourite among the fishermen and the butt of their jokes. Of his Nocturnes, they said he couldn't row out fast enough to catch the sun as it went down.

Vanessa would know of the many sail lofts used as studios, as she strolled in Downlong, the epicentre of the fishing community, its harsh life and work. The influx of artists into the town during the 1880s meant a proliferation of premises rented out as studios to supplement the fishermen's income from the dwindling fishing industry. Some boasted skylights and were large enough to live in. The best and largest of the converted sail lofts lined the beach at Porthmeor and during spring tides the studios would be swamped, not only by gigantic seas, but by mountains of sand pressing against the huge windows.

Vanessa would have noticed that the artists in the town were ladies and gentlemen, setting up their easels and canvas to paint their seascapes. Every year there would be Show Day. The art critic, Lewis Hind, wrote 'More pictures are painted in Cornwall in the course of the year than in any county. The great centres are Newlyn, St Ives and Falmouth, and the votes of the Cornish contingent, it is said, can turn the scale in an election at the Royal Academy.'[17]

Many of these artists visited Talland House: 'Mr & Mrs Titcomb to tea.'

The Titcombs lived at Windy Parc and Stella notes, 'Father and Mr M. to Titcombs then for a walk.' Titcomb painted the fishermen at their work on the harbour. 'Mrs A. Stokes & Mrs Birch to tea.'[18] This would be the artist Marianne Stokes and the other could have been the wife of the artist Lamorna Birch, living in Lamorna Valley. Vanessa may even have met the Finnish artist, Helene Schjerfbeck, now among the foremost artists of that country and friend of Marianne Stokes. Schjerfbeck and Stokes had studied together in Europe and often painted the same subject matter and used the same models, as in *The Convalescent*. The girl was probably a child from the fishing community.

The Convalescent,
Helene Schjerfbeck

Newlyn Artists

Ten miles away at Newlyn, a fishing village beyond the town of Penzance, other fishing families were accommodating artists. At Newlyn Vanessa would have met artists such as Walter Langley, the first major artist to settle there and record with his brush the lives of the fisherfolk. Stanhope and Elizabeth Forbes were prominent in the community. Elizabeth was renowned for her paintings of children and spent much time painting in Percy Craft's studio in St Ives, which she preferred to Newlyn. Stanhope's *Fish Sale on a Cornish Beach*, exhibited at the Royal Academy in 1885, and *The Health of the Bride* shown in 1889, did much to put Newlyn at the forefront of artists painting in this genre.

In 1899 at their home, Higher Faughan, the Forbes established the Newlyn School, famous for paintings of uncompromising realism.

Painting *en plein air* was the newest development in Britain, but it was already prominent in France and Brittany, where most artists from Newlyn and St Ives had been influenced by this technique. Norman Garstin, renowned for his atmospheric painting of Penzance promenade in 1889, *The Rain it Raineth Every Day*, wryly remarked that a painting could not be good unless the artist had caught a cold doing it. This work is owned by the Penzance Charter Trustees and exhibited at Penlee House Museum and Art Gallery, so remains in Cornwall.

In Newlyn artists were using local models, posed in a cottage or on the beach *en plein air*, amid fish and boats, or creating some dramatic scene of distraught and exhausted women, looking out to sea, where dawn offers no hope of a sail nor the return of their menfolk, nor the boat on which their livelihood depended.

Show Day and Julius Olsson

In St Ives the main subject of the paintings was the landscape and the sea in all its changing moods. At the yearly Show Day the population of the town and local schools and hoards of incoming visitors traipsed round the studios to see the paintings, which were destined for judgement by the committee at the Royal Academy. Pictures were framed, packed and transported by the Great Western Railway from Lanham's Gallery to the Royal Academy or Paris Salon. The peak of achievement was to be hung 'on the line' (at eye level) at the RA Summer Exhibition, to be seen by thousands, and perhaps to capture the attention of members of the Chantrey Bequest, who were buying paintings and sculpture to form the nucleus of a National Collection. Vanessa attended the Summer Shows at the RA, where she would recognize the names of many St Ives artists, and as a child would have visited their studios. Indeed, Mr and Mrs Julius Olsson were friends of the Stephen family at Talland House.

*Visitors to studios
at Show Day*

Moonlit Shore, by the seascape painter Julius Olsson, was bought by the Chantrey Bequest in 1911. His paintings were accepted to hang in the Royal Academy 175 times. He was elected a Royal Academician in 1920. Olsson, together with Louis Grier, set up the first School of Landscape and Marine Painting in St Ives in 1895. The advertisement for their school appeared in the St Ives *Weekly Summary:*

Two young artists Mr Louis Grier and Mr Julius Olsson, are announcing the opening in St Ives, Cornwall, of a School of Landscape and Marine Painting. The main idea of this School is to give students an opportunity of studying out of door effects, and therefore the work of students will, weather permitting, be carried on actually in the open air, and will only be taken into the studio when atmospheric conditions render open air painting impossible.[19]

Olsson's studio fronted the Atlantic coast with its huge seas and rolling surf. He was described in *The Studio* magazine as 'a big man with a big heart, who paints big pictures with big brushes in a big studio.'

Julius Olsson in Porthmeor studio

Sickert and Whistler

During the Stephens' long association with St Ives Walter Richard Sickert came to the town, when Vanessa was only five and he, in 1883 at the age of twenty-three, was a student of James McNeill Whistler. They were lodging at Barnoon Terrace, with one of the best views over the town and bay. His father Oswald and brother Bernard, also painters, were visitors in 1897. In 1883 Walter Sickert was already familiar with St Ives. Later, Vanessa came to admire his paintings, and he was very encouraging in her early years as a painter. He talked to her of St Ives and remembered seeing her parents in the town, her father 'the most impressive personage in the area,' and her mother, who 'had looked superb.'[20] He had a lifelong interest in theatre and had acted in Henry Irving's company of players when they toured Cornwall. The actor-manager Sir Henry Irving had been brought up by a Cornish aunt and had spent his boyhood years in Halsetown, a village two miles out of St Ives. He was the first man to be knighted for services to the stage.

Sickert, among other artist friends, floated on the edges of the Bloomsbury Group. In 1934 Vanessa designed the cover for Virginia's book, *Walter Sickert: a Conversation*, published by the Hogarth Press in 1934. She noted 'The life of the lower middle class interests him most – of innkeepers, shop-keepers, music-hall actors and actresses. He seems to care little for the life of the aristocracy whether of birth or of intellect', and Virginia observed 'the intimacy that exists in Sickert's pictures between his people and their rooms. The bed, the chest of drawers, the one picture and the vase on the mantelpiece are all expressive of the owner.'[21] In time Vanessa would encapsulate all these features in her paintings of her own environment.

In St Ives Sickert was mixing his master's paints, cleaning his brushes, and attending to his every whim and mood. Doubtless they sauntered into town and came upon artists struggling with their huge canvases while Whistler was painting on small wooden panels, the size of cigar box lids. Elizabeth Forbes was an admirer of both Whistler and Sickert, much to the annoyance of her husband.

Whistler was known for his nocturnes of the Thames, and seeing Louis Grier and his artist friends equally keen on producing effects of light and evening sunset on the harbour, probably dismissed their attempts, for it is well known that Whistler could not tolerate competition. Louis Grier wrote in ironic tone: 'On fine nights the large doors at the end of the studio would be opened, and then we had a series of nocturnes that would have merited the artistic appreciation of Mr Whistler.'[22]

Vanessa and Virginia as Companions

In London Vanessa and Virginia were furthering their art education by frequent visits to the Royal Academy and other art galleries. In 1897 they saw the exhibition of Lord Leighton's paintings and next day at the National Gallery 'We saw everything – old Italians, Dutches, English and a great room full of Turner water colours.'[23] A few days later they paid a visit to the New Gallery, Regent Street, which was exhibiting George Frederic Watts's paintings in celebration of his eightieth birthday.

The artist had lived for over twenty years at Little Holland House, Kensington, the home of Julia's aunt. Ottoline Morrell described Vanessa 'as beautiful as a Watts painting,' which is unfortunate; Vanessa had little regard for Watts as a painter. She considered he had wasted his talent, neglecting the art of painting and using it only as a half-learned language.[24] The remark is typical of the art student who wishes to push the boundaries of art to reflect the spirit of the time.

Nessa and Ginnie were good and constant companions. They often worked together, one painting or drawing, the other either reading to herself, or reading aloud. They walked together to Kensington Gardens and skated on the Round Pond when it was frozen over, where 'a chatty old gentleman talked to Nessa of St Ives . . . and cricket.'[25] Virginia recorded meticulously Vanessa's attendance at her painting lessons: 'Nessa went to her studio' begins a diary entry for every Monday, Wednesday and Friday. 'Nessa had to walk down to the studio because of the wind. She brought me back *North and South*, [Mrs Gaskell] which I shall read out aloud to Nessa.'[26] She also read aloud Dickens's *David Copperfield*. 'Nessa went to have her lunch at an ABC near the studio, so as to get in as much drawing as possible. I walked to Kensington Square and then to the studio, to fetch Nessa back.'[27]

Virginia wrote of how often they were together in their activities. In Brighton 'Nessa and I sat on the beach – Nessa attempting a picture of the Pier, & I reading *Barchester Towers* [Anthony Trollope] to myself.'[28] In Gloucester, 'In the afternoon we went for a walk to an old house which Nessa painted, a house with lions on the gate posts & a sun dial.'[29] At Painswick, 'She [Nessa] is painting from the summer house,'[30] and 'Nessa painted a little down at the bottom of the garden.

Nessa painting and I reading.'[31]

The sisters attempted to instruct girls less fortunate than themselves, namely a group of six working women, meeting them on the steps of the National Gallery and taking them 'laboriously through the Early Italians . . . how far pictures are intelligible to them – I don't know. It is hard work.'[32]

As well as their walks in Kensington Gardens, the sisters often took bus trips up to Hampstead, where the sisters had contact with many other painters and writers. It was here that Vanessa visited Mark Gertler in his Hampstead studio. She told Ottoline Morrell 'He's painting a great picture of a merry-go-round [now owned by the Tate], but he won't let us see it till it's finished. He came to lunch the other day and was very amusing and intelligent. I liked him, and he's so interested in his painting he can hardly talk of anything else, which I rather like,'[33] On Hampstead Heath, 'this little vision of country,' Vanessa and Virginia could tramp for miles over the heath, and from the highest point at Whitestone Pond, they could look out over London and beyond to the Surrey hills.

Art and Artists

Vanessa was also having lessons from Margaret Flower, a painter, who instructed her in art history by visiting the various galleries. At the Grafton Gallery in 1897 they saw the work of Ford Madox Brown and had the good fortune to meet William Holman Hunt, who showed them round and talked about the paintings. William, a member of the Pre-Raphaelite Brotherhood, had first visited Cornwall in 1860 with the painter Val Prinsep, a relative of Julia Stephen. Vanessa was familiar with Hunt's son, Hilary, born the same year as Vanessa, and his sister Gladys, from the days when they, too, spent summer holidays in St Ives. In 1892 the St Ives Visitors' List reported that Mrs Holman Hunt and party were staying at 5 The Terrace. Indeed, the ten-year-old Virginia Stephen recalls in her *Hyde Park Gate News* of August 1892:

Mrs Hunt and her daughter and son arrived at the terminus of St Ives on Wednesday. Mrs and Miss Vanessa Stephen went down to see them arrive. They came the train not being even half an hour late. They went up quickly to their lodgins [sic] which had been engaged for them by Mrs Stephen.[34]

1897 was a good year for artists in St Ives, thirty of whom had their work accepted and hung in the Annual Summer Exhibition at the RA. It was reported in the local paper: 'The old town by the Cornish sea is represented in every room in Burlington House. We cannot doubt that St Ives will now be more firmly established than ever as the most successful and popular Art resort in the West of England.'[35]

*Judging the pictures
at the Royal
Academy*

The visual arts in all its forms were of interest to Vanessa. In 1897 a new camera was bought and tested out on holiday. Stella and her brothers were well versed in taking photographs. In 1892 Virginia recalled that 'She [Miss Stillman] was photographed incessantly by Miss Stella Duckworth and Mr Gerald Duckworth who keep a visitor's list by photographing everyone who comes to the palatial residence.'[36]

Virginia was referring to Talland House. Their great aunt, Julia Margaret Cameron, was a professional portraitist, but Vanessa's camera records informally the family, and visits of friends, as compiled by Quentin Bell and Angelica Garnett in the book *Vanessa Bell's Family Album*. Virginia wrote of their adventures with the camera at Bognor:

We tried shutting Nessa up in the cupboard to put in the films, but there were too many chinks. Then she suggested being covered by her quilt, and everything else that I could lay hands on - she was accordingly, buried in dresses and dressing gowns till no light could penetrate. Soon she emerged almost stifled having forgotten how to put the film in.[37]

This was eventually achieved and she took photos of Stella and Jack on the sands. Back home at Hyde Park Gate, in the night nursery, Nessa and Ginnie developed ten successful photos.

The Royal Academy School

Vanessa's experience of the rich and fertile grounding in art as a child in St Ives, where there was 'an artist on every corner,' must have given her confidence in her own ability to succeed as a painter. In 1901 she applied to study at the Royal Academy School. She wrote to her brother Thoby 'I have been at the studio all today where I am drawing my Academy figure. It's very dull and I'm doing it very badly, so I don't expect I shall even get my first drawings accepted. I don't know where I shall hide my head then.'[38] But her drawings were good enough and she was accepted. Later she was to despise the RA's staid, traditional, Victorian, and unchanging attitude to modern art.

Following this success, she submitted the drawings for a competition at her old school, Mr Cope's School of Art in South Kensington, and was awarded a medal. On three days a week Vanessa left Virginia to her reading and studies, and bicycled off in a large floppy hat and a long skirt. She rarely missed a day. Cope's school was geared to training students for entry to the Royal Academy. The RA Schools had for the past ten years allowed women students to study 'from the partially draped female figure'. The probationary year was a test to 'weed out' the less capable candidates:

The first advantage will be the exclusion of the ordinary run of the lady students, as only the best of them will be equal to the new and more painter-like test. For those of them who succeed in the preliminary examination the new regulation – that of permitting them to study flesh-painting from the semi-nude – is a boon.[39]

Leslie Stephen wrote with pride to a relation in 1902: 'The chief event of this week is that Nessa has been passed into the upper school of the academy. It is good because, I fancy, she was getting rather bored with the eternal drawing from casts & will now have to paint some heads'.[40] Only the best of the female students passed their probationary year and many of her special friends failed. One of these was Margery Snowden (known as Snow), who remained a lifelong correspondent and admiring friend. Vanessa practiced portraiture on Margery, although these seem not to have survived. In the best tradition of students of art, Vanessa continued to study paintings and attend exhibitions. In 1903 she and Virginia were invited to 'an artistic party,' the Royal Academy's annual reception at Burlington House. Virginia commented wryly:

We drifted about, gazing at human pictures mostly, with snatches of desultory talk. We looked with admiration at those ladies, who are the high aristocrats of such gatherings as these – who know the President & all the more distinguished academicians. Their demeanour is beautiful . . . I am always impressed by the splendid superiority of these artist men and women over their Philistine brethren.[41]

Vanessa was fortunate in having parents who encouraged their children's achievements, even though the female members had no formal education in their early years, unlike the males, who went to school. This support must have given Vanessa more confidence in her ability than many young women of her class. Her father, in his early relationship with Julia, tells her that women ought to be as well educated as men and not waste their lives. They should study and be able to work at any profession. In talking of his daughter Laura, but this also would have applied to Vanessa, he wrote to Julia '...if she showed any taste for drawing she should go to the best teachers and cultivate it thoroughly, as if she meant to make a profession of it and not a mere amusement.'[42]

Vanessa enjoyed studying for three years at the Royal Academy Schools from 1901-1904. She wrote to her friend Margery:

. . . [John Singer] Sargent is teaching most extraordinarily well at the RA. How I wish you were there. . . . He insists upon thick paint and makes one try get the right tone at once – apparently the drawing is to be got entirely by painting thickly the different tones. The one thing he is down upon is when he thinks anyone is trying for an effect regardless of truth.[43]

Even Sargent, mild-mannered compared to Tonks, had crushed and 'subdued' several of the women students by his criticism: 'Of course there are many minor lights whom he squashes I don't think anyone has had any praise.'[44]

A Brief Study at the Slade

After completing her studies at the Royal Academy Vanessa applied to study at the Slade School of Drawing, Painting and Sculpture. Here she met Philip Wilson Steer, Professor Frederick Brown, and Professor Henry Tonks, who regarded it almost as a duty to scare off the number of females anxious to study with them.

In 1900 Vanessa was innocent of the fact that some of her future tormentors of her student days at the Slade School of Art, Frederick

Brown and Philip Wilson Steer, were in St Ives. They were staying at Chy-an-Porth, opposite the Porthminster Hotel, the home of the local artist Moffat Lindner, whose paintings of Venice and St Ives seascapes were closer to Impressionism than many of his St Ives contemporaries. Chy-an-Porth is situated to the left of Talland House and can be seen from its balconies. While in St Ives Steer painted a portrait of Lindner's wife Augusta. She was also a painter, and came to St Ives to study under Julius Olsson, but gave up when her husband's work commanded more favourable attention from the critics.

The Slade had opened in 1871 and was run by practising artists who placed emphasis on working from the figure, as in the French *ateliers*. There was a Women's Life Room, where studies were made of draped models who posed every day, and in fact they also had mixed life classes. At one time women students outnumbered men. Two important contemporary women painters who had also studied at the Slade were Gwen John in 1895 and Dora Carrington in 1910 (the latter, one of the women artists who had bobbed their hair, named crop-heads, by Virginia). There were also Sylvia Frances Milman, Winifred Knights, Ethel Walker, Nina Hamnett, Iris Tree, Dorothy Brett, Barbara Hiles-Bagenal. There, too, were Dod Procter, who afterwards studied and lived in Newlyn, and Margery Mostyn who, with her husband Leonard Fuller established a School of Painting in St Ives in 1938.

Tonks had taught, or rather 'squashed', Vanessa. She also felt intimidated by artists of the New English Art Club, whose members all seemed to have 'the secret of the universe within their grasp, a secret one was not worthy to learn, especially if one was that terrible low creature, a female painter.'[45] In the early years of the twentieth century it was still difficult for females to get an art education; training was simplest for the daughters of artists, who were familiar with a studio.

In November 1904 Vanessa began work at the Slade. In December she hadn't 'dared to show my works to Tonks yet.' But by January 1905 she had decided she was wasting her time there. She had, after all, completed her training at the RA and wanted to move on, rather than repeat the process. However, in spite of complaining of the various knocks she received to her confidence by the harshness of Henry Tonks, surprisingly, she invited him to her studio at Gordon Square to view and criticise her paintings. After some time he did arrive, and Virginia noted the nervousness of Vanessa waiting for him 'in great misery' to pass judgement, which he did with a good deal of severity but also 'some praise'. Vanessa was also keen to obtain a critique from John Singer Sargent, her former tutor, whose studio she visited, and who remembered her from the RA Schools. He was a Royal Academician and a renowned portrait painter of the rich, famous and aristocratic. Vanessa must indeed have trembled at his approach.

Bernard Leach

One other connection with Vanessa's student days and St Ives was the tall slender figure of a man who became a student at the Slade, during the few months Vanessa was there. This fellow student was Bernard Leach. His drawing of a nude is marked on the back in his handwriting 'My first drawing from the nude at the Slade, 1903.' Did they ever meet, I wonder? - although I learn from Vanessa's writing that she 'made no friends there and soon left.'[46] Bernard Leach studied drawing with Henry Tonks at the Slade, and etching with Frank Brangwyn at the London School of Art. Brangwyn was an early member of the St Ives colony, and among the first exhibitors in the new art gallery established in St Ives by James Lanham in 1889.

In 1920 Bernard Leach, who had studied pottery in Japan, and his Japanese friend Shoji Hamada, established the Leach Pottery in St Ives, and rediscovered the craft of English slipware. They built the first Japanese climbing kiln in Europe. Leach also believed in teaching students by workshop methods and in developing their skills in handling clay, from mixing, shaping on the wheel, firing pots to working in the showroom. The Leach Pottery is a renowned place of pilgrimage

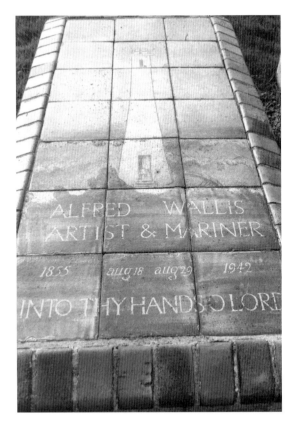

for students of ceramics from around the world. The artist, Patrick Heron, a conscientious objector during the second world war, was detailed to work at the Leach Pottery.

Bernard Leach is responsible for the unique gravestone of Alfred Wallis, St Ives's most renowned primitive artist. Wallis, a semi-literate, retired fisherman, took up painting at the age of seventy. The quality of his paintings was recognised by Ben Nicholson and Christopher Wood when they walked past the old fisherman's cottage in Back Road West in 1928.

Wallis's paintings now hang in the Tate Gallery, alongside those of Nicholson and Wood, without whose active promotion the old man would have died in obscurity, with other primitive artists of his class.

Leach tiles on Alfred Wallis's grave

St Ives harbour, Godrevy and Seine boats, *Alfred Wallis*

Vanessa Avoids being the Angel in the House

When Vanessa took over the management of the house at Hyde Park Gate, after the deaths of her mother and stepsister Stella, she was beset by family and domestic problems. She must have looked back to those carefree childhood years in St Ives, when her main social duty was entertaining her parents' many visitors to Talland House, often taking them down to Porthminster beach. Their life was recorded by Stella in her diary of 1893: 'Lovely bathing. Adrian swam quite a good way. Nessa & I painted honeysuckle in Rose Garden,'[47] or they played cricket in the garden. 'Children and I blackberried . . . came back late for tea to find Dick & Rupert [Brooke] waiting for cricket.' Then there were visits to the shops: 'Mother (& Mr Headlam of course) went to the town.' There were various country walks undertaken by Virginia and her father but more reluctantly by Vanessa who, like Lily Briscoe in Virginia's novel, *To the Lighthouse*, preferred to sit and sketch in the garden looking out to Godrevy lighthouse, the sea and Hayle Towans, the lonely sand dunes behind the three miles of Hayle beach.

How did an eighteen-year-old girl manage to fulfil her demanding new role? The practicalities of life must almost have overwhelmed her, especially with the extra demands made upon her by Virginia's nervous breakdown; but she had her escape route, her art. It was indeed this preoccupation with art, which Vanessa doggedly followed when expected to be 'the Angel in the House', that saved her from being tied to the life of self-sacrifice demanded by a Victorian father:

When I got into the grubby, shabby, dirty world of art students . . . I wanted nothing else in the way of society. They were separate entirely from my home life and so a great relief . . . in their company one could forget oneself and think of nothing but shapes and colours and the absorbing difficulties of oil paint.[48]

After the death of Leslie Stephen, Vanessa was free to move into the modern world and to make her own decisions without recourse to her father, or her stepbrothers. From the constraints of her father's household

Vanessa seems to have taken a giant leap into the new century. As decision-maker, in the years between 1897 and her father's death in 1904, she had learnt enough of household management to enable her to move the Stephen family from their home at Hyde Park Gate into the lighter, brighter house at 46 Gordon Square in Bloomsbury. She also took the family to Europe. In Venice they spent their mornings seeing pictures, and the afternoons churches. In Florence she bought old picture frames, very cheap, and nicer than any she could buy in London. In Paris they visited Rodin's studio and met many contemporary painters. It was in Paris that Vanessa came to know her brother Thoby's friend, Clive Bell.

Back to St Ives

In 1905 Vanessa, Virginia, Thoby and Adrian made a nostalgic and sentimental train journey back to their childhood home at St Ives. Vanessa admitted that she 'likes train journeys you know.' She was also escaping the attentions of Clive Bell, who had proposed marriage to her for the second time. She wrote in a letter to her friend Margery

. . . when one is actually asked by a man to marry him, even though one has no feeling at all of that kind oneself, one is obliged to think rather more seriously about it than one has done before . . . I should be quite happy living with anyone whom I didn't dislike . . . if I could paint and lead the kind of life I like. [49]

Virginia tramped around the countryside in all weathers and Vanessa painted. 'Vanessa, in Cornwall, painted several small seascapes, employing Whistler's method, using a red or brown base to deepen the blues of sea and sky.'[50] These paintings were perhaps lost in the bombing of the Fitzroy Street studio in 1940.

Vanessa wished her friend Margery could be with her in Cornwall. She wrote that the house was new and hideous and the furniture awful, 'but the place is most beautiful.' Vanessa felt she had never been away, and noted how everything was the same. She was determined to use her time painting as much as she could:

You can't imagine the colour of the sea here. It is quite unlike any other, and the country altogether is beautiful, very wild and bare. I mean to paint a great deal. I have established myself in my room much as we did in our hotels and mean to paint sunsets from the window. We look out across the bay, and the sun sets just behind the headland to the left, so that one gets most lovely effects on the sea. [51]

Virginia wrote from Trevose House, Carbis Bay that she writes all morning while Vanessa paints all afternoon, pronouncing that her sister was working very hard and achieved some of her best work. 'Nessa produces two canvases a day; and is mad with the difficulties of the sea.'[52]

Now that Vanessa's painting career had begun, and with all the influences she gained from European artists, she seriously thought about her painting techniques and how they were to be achieved: should she paint thickly on a new canvas and try at once to achieve the right tone and colour, as advised by Sargent, or should she follow the example of Whistler and paint thinly, layer upon layer, building up to the final surface. This was a problem that engaged Vanessa's thoughts and in a lecture some years later she was to tell students: 'It is indeed so exciting

Boats at Anchor 1905, *John Park*

and so absorbing, this painters' world of form and colour, that once you are at its mercy you are in grave danger of forgetting all other aspects of the material world.'[53]

While in St Ives did Vanessa perhaps see the Fauvist paintings of John Park and Hayley Lever? - They were briefly influenced by this new movement circulating in Paris for thick applications of paint, with heightened colour defining the subject matter. John Park's heavy impasto painting of the harbour is quite unlike his usual thin reflective, translucent colours.

Bloomsbury

Back in Gordon Square, the four young people of the Stephen family, Thoby, Virginia and Adrian, under the direction of Vanessa, set about lightening the rooms in which they were to live. The walls bounced light from pale colours and their faces shone into the room. Gone were the heavy William Morris wallpapers and sombre colours. Vanessa recalls the solemnity of Hyde Park Gate 'At dinner in the evening faces loomed out of the surrounding shade like Rembrandt portraits. . . .'[54]

Their one link with the past came through Sophie Farrell, their cook from Hyde Park Gate and St Ives. Sophie maintained a lifelong attachment to the Stephen family, remembering their childhood games and adventures in the summers at St Ives. In a letter she wrote at the age of seventy-four she quotes her involvement with the various members of the Stephen family as spanning fifty years. One wonders whether it was in St Ives she was first taken on as a cook, Farrell being a local St Ives name.

In Bloomsbury a group of like-minded artists and writers, who lived within the area, frequently gathered at the home of the Stephens. Many were friends of Thoby from his days at Cambridge. Among the early members were Lytton Strachey, Maynard Keynes and Clive Bell, joined by Roger Fry, Duncan Grant, Morgan Forster, Leonard Woolf, and others over a number of years, but their meetings petered out with the First World War. However, in spite of Vanessa denying there ever was a group known as Bloomsbury, it remains a name with which we associate certain individuals.

The First Commission and the New English Art Club

Perhaps in opposition to the mainly literary predominance of the Thursday meetings in Gordon Square, Vanessa set up a society of painters known as the Friday Club, and within a month had organised their first exhibition and shown three of her paintings. Five years on the Friday Club was still operating. She noted a young man of seventeen who she marked down as promising. He was Mark Gertler: 'I think he may be going to be good.' He studied at the Slade and fell in love with an elusive fellow student, Dora Carrington. Other Slade students at this time were Paul Nash, Stanley Spencer and Ben Nicholson.

In January 1905 Virginia noted in her diary: 'Snow to sit to Nessa.' Shortly afterwards, she was engaged on a painting of Lady Robert Cecil. The following month we hear of the progress of the portrait. 'Nessa painting Nelly, who sits now in her own drawing room, by the window, with a green curtain & Troper [her dog] at her feet.'[55]

Vanessa finally left her student days behind with her first exhibition, in 1905, at the New Gallery, London, at which she showed her first commissioned portrait of Nelly (Lady Cecil). The four Stephen children visited the exhibition many times to celebrate Vanessa's success:

April 1905. A morning devoted to art! – happily successful. I went off after breakfast to the New Gallery which might or might not have hung the Nelly picture – & to my great relief found it in the Catalogue, & saw it hang fairly in the gallery, which is quite a cheerful beginning. Dashed home & general rejoicing of a mild description. Went in the afternoon with Adrian & Nessa (most unwillingly) to the show again. [56]

The following year Vanessa was engaged to paint the portrait of Lord Robert, and a further commission from a Mrs Seton to paint portraits of her children. Her great concern in these early years was to please her sitters and achieve a likeness. The New Gallery at which Vanessa exhibited her work was none other than the New English Art Club, which she had railed against, when she was a student, for their superior attitude.

William Henry Bartlett, Henry Scott Tuke and Thomas Cooper Gotch, three artists associated with St Ives, Falmouth and Newlyn, proposed the founding of the new English Art Club in 1886. Others were Frederick Brown, John Singer Sargent and W.J. Laidlay, who was their first chairman. Other St Ives artist members were Thomas Millie Dow, later of Talland House, Henry Detmold, Adrian Stokes, Marianne Stokes, Sir

Alfred East, Julius Olsson, William Holt Yates Titcomb, and Moffat Lindner. In the early years the painters felt they had joined an egalitarian society in which members possessed no privileges of rank, and work was judged and accepted on its merits, without personal bias or the chancy competition of the Royal Academy.

Vanessa was exhibiting in the same gallery as more recognized and established artists, among them John Singer Sargent. This was a great achievement for a twenty-six year old only recently out of art school.

Vanessa Marries

Vanessa was preoccupied with Clive's persistence in pursuing her with his second proposal of marriage. She asked him to go away, 'I thought for a year.' He spent some time at his family home, engaging in the hunting, shooting and fishing activities so despised by Vanessa. However, fate pointed circumstances in Clive's direction when in 1906 her beloved brother Thoby died. They had returned to Gordon Square from a trip to Greece; both were ill, but while Vanessa recovered, Thoby died of typhoid fever.

Clive and Vanessa consoled each other over this death, united in their grief through their love of Thoby, and one feels Vanessa accepted Clive's third proposal of marriage in a desperate effort to evade the spectre of death that had pursued her in the last few years. Also, she could talk endlessly about Thoby, one of Clive's closest friends. They married at St Pancras Registry Office in February 1907, and went at once to Paris.

From Paris Vanessa wrote to her friend Margery: 'we have asked a young artist called Duncan Grant to dine with us. We both knew him before we came here as he is a cousin of the Stracheys. He is clever and very nice. I hope we shall see him in London quite often when he goes back there.'[57] This would appear to be the first stirrings of Vanessa's attraction to Duncan Grant. It also proved a difficult time for Vanessa. She had not been able to paint but informed Margery 'Now I mean to have models and work hard at painting some nudes and perhaps one or two portraits.'[58]

St Ives Again

Following their first successful visit to St Ives, three years later in 1908 Virginia, followed by Vanessa, Clive and baby Julian, travelled on the Great Western Railway from Paddington to alight at St Ives station. Vanessa had sent instructions to Virginia:

Don't give up the best bedroom, for you will want it to sit in probably and Clive and I shall want separate rooms. He tried here sleeping in the dressing room, but gave it up as he couldn't get to sleep again after once being waked by Julian. We shall get to St Ives at 7.10 on Friday. Will you order a short vehicle to bring me and the nurse and baby from the station with one box and perambulator, and unless they should arrive beforehand also another two boxes, Julian's cradle and bath? [59]

They lodged at Trevose House, Draycott Terrace, from which there is a fine view of the town and harbour. Mrs Proudfoot, a St Ives woman who was a child at the time, remembers the occasion when Virginia arrived: 'In 1908 Miss Stephen lodged with my mother. She came to St Ives on her own. She went walking on the moors. She was a bit of an eccentric.' [60] She remembered nothing of the arrival of Vanessa. There was also a Trevose House at Carbis Bay where they stayed. The houses were named from Trevose lighthouse, which lies further north-east on the Cornish coast.

Trevose House, Draycott Terrace, St Ives

Virginia returned from this holiday before the Bells and Vanessa wrote to her sister that they had come struggling back from the beach, all uphill, where she had been sketching the sea, and Virginia's dog had interrupted the games of a family of children. She was ironical about what Virginia must have been thinking of her preoccupation with the baby, and the domesticity attached to motherhood.

Indeed, it was at this time that a flirtation took place between Virginia and Clive, both it is thought, pushed to the background by Vanessa's preoccupation with the infant Julian. Virginia and Clive were ostensibly consoling each other for Vanessa's neglect of them. It is an indication of the pivotal role that Vanessa played in the circle of friends that surrounded her.

Vanessa's daughter Angelica Garnett, in her autobiography *Deceived with Kindness* some years later, remarks how her mother was the magnetic centre of the household at their long term home of Charleston, whether at the dining table, or in her studio:

. . . Vanessa was self-reliant almost to a fault, producing an effect of rocklike stability that was not as secure as it seemed. For the rest of her life she spent a large part of her energy in creating and maintaining a circle of safety, within which she could gather together all the elements she most loved and depended on. Her mother's early death may well have stimulated a fear of the outside world and a deep need of family life.[61]

After the brief flirtation of Virginia and Clive, stable relations seemed restored by March 1909, when Vanessa wrote to Virginia from the Lizard, in Cornwall. She described the countryside on their walks and the effects of light breaking through a grey sky, and how the subject would be tackled by various painters and how they would have portrayed the scene, but her attempts to capture the moment were disappointing to her. 'I flattered myself that I saw how it ought to be treated but I could not do it. A melancholy watercolour of a sunset is my only achievement.'[62]

Later, at Cleeve House, Clive's family home, Vanessa was cast down by the family's inability to talk of nothing but the weather, or dogs and shooting. She deplored their dull conversation and wasting their lives doing nothing. In such tedious company she felt 'clever and almost a genius.' She found it impossible to paint in such an arid atmosphere and envied Virginia: 'what is one to do in Wiltshire while you are sniffing the smells of St Ives?'[63]

By September 1909, Vanessa was at Studland Bay, near Poole Harbour, in more invigorating company. She had invited Lytton Strachey to join them, and Virginia came too. This was one of a number of visits to Dorset which led to her producing one of her most ambitious and experimental works.

The painting *Studland Beach* is engaged with itself. Two seated figures in the foreground, with their backs to the onlooker, but looking very like Virginia and Vanessa's son Julian, sit watching a group on the edge of the sea, where four children are intent upon some occupation with the sand. A woman standing with her back to the viewer looks as though

Studland Beach
1912, *Vanessa Bell*

she is about to enter a canvas bathing tent, very like the Victorian tents on Porthmeor beach in St Ives. Long swathes of colour sweep down from the left hand corner and give the painting an abstract quality, whilst there is also an obscure narrative element going on in the picture. Richard Shone described *Studland Beach* 'as one of the most radical paintings in England for its date.'[64]

Post-Impressionist Exhibitions 1910 and 1912

Roger Fry's exhibition of 1910, Manet and the Post-Impressionists, at the Grafton Gallery caused shock waves through the art establishment. Fry predicted that he thought the show would be a 'great affair' and he was preparing himself 'for a huge campaign of outraged British Philistinism.' He was not wrong in his predictions. Vanessa was convinced that no other single exhibition had more effect on the younger generation of painters, and the shocking sensation experienced by the traditionalists only added to the fun and exhilaration. 'That autumn of 1910 is to me a time when everything seemed springing to new life – a time when all was a sizzle of excitement, new relationships, new ideas, different and intense emotions all seemed crowding into one's life.'[65]

While Vanessa was thrilling to the opening up of everything in the art world, she was at the same time a worried mother. It was in 1910 that Quentin was born, and failing to gain weight after the birth. Her friend Margery Snowden came for a month to help nurse Vanessa back to health and strength.

Vanessa was excited by the first Post-Impressionist Exhibition: 'it was there I first saw a work by Cezanne, one that impressed me without my knowing why, of bare trees and house and water in front . . . and I remember a very lovely little Van Gogh of flowers in a jug.'[66] For Vanessa it was 'a sudden revelation and encouragement'.

Here the British public had the opportunity to view the work of Cezanne, Matisse, Picasso, Van Gogh, and Gauguin; painters who influenced her with their colourful and lyrical work. There were a few

English painters she admired: Sickert, Augustus John, Steer and Sargent, but even then she thought their best work was behind them. At an exhibition in 1911 she expressed her opinion that Miss Gwen John was 'more interesting than anyone', a view expressed by many in recent times. She felt the future of painting lay with the French artists.

During this time Vanessa and Roger Fry became close. She found him a stimulating and interesting companion. They could talk art and exchange ideas. He introduced her to the world of art dealers. Even then Roger realised the artist and designer in Vanessa and knew he could never achieve the lyrical compositions of her paintings. He was critic, appreciative admirer, entrepreneur, and someone who could move things forward by his enthusiasm and energy. He fell in love with Vanessa during the time he nursed her through a serious miscarriage in 1911, when she, Clive and Roger were travelling in Turkey.

Meanwhile, Clive was involved in his own affairs of the heart, and Duncan Grant was in a relationship with Vanessa's brother Adrian. In the free-thinking-and-acting circle of Bloomsbury, the frequency of mix and match partnerships was normal and occurred without critical disapproval.

For the second Post-Impressionist exhibition of 1912 Vanessa helped with the hanging, and noted there were thirty works of Matisse to be displayed, as well as works by Picasso. French, English and Russian artists were all represented. Vanessa exhibited three works, and Stanley Spencer, who later spent his honeymoon in St Ives but was then still a student, had his painting *John Donne Arriving in Heaven* selected and hung; this in defiance of Henry Tonks's advice to his students at the Slade to stay away from the contamination of the Grafton Gallery. Leonard Woolf, recently married to Virginia, manned this exhibition and reported that large numbers of people came to the show: 'nine out of ten of them either roared with laughter at the pictures or were enraged by them.'[67] However, Roger Fry expressed his gratitude that Professor Fred Brown, also of the Slade, had been converted to the ideas embodied in the paintings.

Vanessa's Painting Bought for the Nation

Vanessa was already well into her painting career by 1912, when she wrote to her husband: 'Dearest, I have a most astonishing piece of news to give you. I have sold a picture! Doesn't that startle you? And you will be still more astonished when you hear who has bought it. The Contemporary Art Fund!'[68] The Contemporary Art Society purchased works by British artists, which were then given or loaned to public collections. The painting was *The Spanish Model*, first exhibited along with three other of her pictures at the second Post-Impressionist exhibition. The visitors had come to the studio at 46 Gordon Square to purchase a work by Duncan Grant but as that particular painting was not available, they had chosen one of hers. This was incredible to Vanessa, who was ambivalent about her status as a professional artist. Her day, as with so many women, was broken up by important fragments of time with her two sons and other household responsibilities. She wrote from Asheham House, shared by Virginia with Vanessa and her family:

. . . I give Julian his reading lesson! . . . then I have to talk a little to Quentin, and then perhaps I paint, when curtain-making allows of it, but I haven't really embarked on much painting yet. Julian has lunch with me, which means that it takes about one-and-a-half hours, and I can't settle down to write letters after lunch, and then you see comes tea and the children again, and then I read my Times *of yesterday and after dinner all the important letters have to be written and then in odd moments there is my dog!'* [69]

Vanessa, in spite of her myriad duties to children and household, managed an active life of painting of canvases, murals, and decorative schemes, and exhibitions and travelling to Europe to study painting and meet other painters. In one of Vanessa's exhibitions in the 1930s, her most successful period, she sold twelve pictures. She was amazed. 'I think it's largely because of *The Times* article today.' The article was written by Charles Marriott, at one time resident in St Ives and then art critic for *The Times* and other art publications.

The Early Paintings of Vanessa

Vanessa's bold areas of colour in her 1911-'12 painting *Virginia Woolf* show her quick, free use of the brush to provide outline, with infill blocks of colour. Features are hinted at. In a further study of 1912, *Virginia Woolf in a Deckchair*, there are no distinguishing facial features. She is to become even looser in her compositions when she merges colour and form. Now, with the merest of outlines for guidance, Vanessa uses her colour freely, fluidly and with confidence, especially so in *Lytton Strachey*, 1913. She places her colour instinctively, dissolving form, enjoying laying the pigment on the canvas and exploring areas with her brush. It is a work in the style of the Fauvists. Duncan Grant and Roger Fry, painted Lytton at the same time but 'Bell's is by far the most vivid and successful painting, showing the future author in his Augustus John phase.'[70]

It is clear from these early paintings that Vanessa was a modernist painter and ahead of her time. She broke new ground with her ideas of form, line, and colour. These radical works should have earned her a place in art history. However, she was not ambitious for critical acclaim, and being a woman, she did not receive it. But having made her mark, she moved on. Those experts who searched for the visionary painters failed to acknowledge Vanessa. Perhaps it is now too embarrassing to admit that art historians have overlooked her contribution to the foundation of modern British art? But why, since there was no avant-garde tradition in England, was she not recognised?

In Vanessa's brief dalliance with abstraction and with the idea of moving art away from the confines of tradition and reliance on the art of drawing, as taught at the Slade, the influences of the artists of Europe, and the Post-Impressionist exhibitions had flooded into her psyche and re-emerged in her own language of paint. Through this she is discovering her own pathway. Vanessa, Duncan Grant and Roger Fry were no longer 'under the Victorian cloud.' The freshness of approach to painting by Cezanne, Bonnard, Pissarro, Van Gogh, Gauguin, and Matisse was a release for their own inventiveness.

Indeed, this early experimentation in abstraction, though short-lived, was the first wave of modernism before Ben Nicholson's generation.

Abstract painting 1912, *Vanessa Bell*

One would assume, too, that Nicholson, along with other recalcitrant students at the Slade, would have seen the work in Roger Fry's Post-Impressionist exhibitions, especially since these drew the derision of their tutors at the Slade. Ben Nicholson's first abstract painting was dated 1924. Vanessa's abstract paintings preceded his by twelve years.

William Rothenstein noted the early signs of Vanessa's rejection of the art of the past masters:

I was asked to make a pastel portrait of Leslie Stephen . . . for Trinity Hall, Cambridge, his old College. Vanessa Stephen was then studying at the Slade School. Pre-Raphaelitism was by now forgotten, and she impressed me, when I met her in houses where the older ideas still lingered, with the quiet courage of her opinions. She looked as though she might have walked among the fair women of Burne-Jones's Golden Stairs; but she spoke with the voice of Gauguin. [71]

In 1917-'18 Vanessa's painting of *The Tub* characterised the end of a series of works she had produced up to that time. She also produced a woodcut of *The Tub* in 1919 for the Omega Workshops. A woman stands naked beside a bath of water. The subject of the painting was Mary Hutchinson, Clive Bell's present girl friend, yet it was likened by Angelica to a self-portrait symbolising loneliness. Vanessa wrote to Roger Fry 'I've been working at my big bath picture and am rather excited about that. 'I've taken out the woman's chemise and in consequence she is quite nude and much more decent.'[72]

If Angelica Bell is correct that the picture symbolizes loneliness, then perhaps we can attribute this loneliness to the all too brief affair Vanessa had with Duncan Grant, which resulted in the birth of their daughter, Angelica, at Christmas in 1918. Soon after the birth sexual relations ceased between the two, by agreement, but obviously at Duncan's insistence. But at least Vanessa had finally persuaded Duncan to sleep with her. Duncan declined to own the child as his own, and the complicity of the three in claiming Angelica as the child of Clive

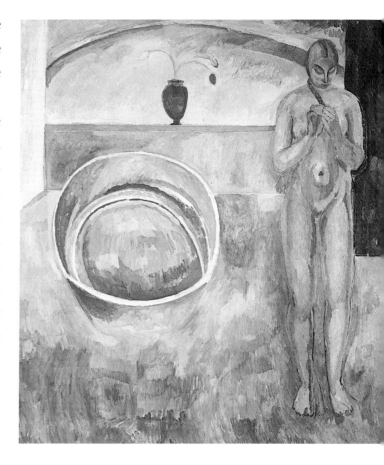

The Tub 1917,
Vanessa Bell

seems uncharacteristic of people who cared so little for other people's opinions and morality. One can only assume that Duncan did not want to accept the responsibility of being a father, or to have the title cluttering up his chosen lifestyle. Vanessa must have been hurt by this double rejection, and certainly Angelica was upset when the truth was revealed to her at the age of eighteen.

Looking at the work of both Duncan and Vanessa, she is the equal artist, but at the time it was Duncan whose reputation was the greater. Roger Fry's painting is governed by the outlines he uses which restrict his colour and his subject matter. His work therefore is more restrained. Vanessa found difficulty in praising his work. Roger's advice to her was not to paint the same subject matter as Duncan, whether still life or portrait, and therefore invite unfavourable comparison. But Vanessa and

Duncan were comfortable painting together. 'We talk of hardly anything but painting.' Indeed, in Fry's exhibition of 1921, *Nameless*, in which all the exhibitors were anonymous, Henry Tonks mistook a painting by Vanessa for a Duncan Grant. Vanessa was surprised and flattered, but Tonks compounded his mistake and his prejudice by giving a little lecture on how pitiful it was that women always imitated men.

Omega Workshops

Fired by his enthusiasm that had been aroused by mounting the two Post-Impressionist exhibitions, Roger Fry developed the Omega Workshops at 33 Fitzroy Square in 1913, catering for every domestic decorative requirement for the home from pictures, pottery, screens, carpets, furniture, curtains to ladies' fashion. Ottoline Morrell supported the Omega Workshops by buying hand-printed materials from their showroom. Vanessa Bell and Duncan Grant were part of the management team, with Jessie Etchells, Winifred Gill, Dora Carrington, Barbara Hiles Bagenal, Dorothy Brett and others producing some of the work. There was also a room design for an Ideal Home stand, with geometric patterns and straight lines in Art Deco style. (In 1916 Vanessa held her first solo show on the premises at 33 Fitzroy Square.)

In this year of 1913 we see Vanessa turning more and more away from Roger and trying to transfer her affections to Duncan. She prefers to sketch and paint quietly with him, and not engage in intellectual talk and analysis of paintings with Roger. Also she prefers Duncan's work to Roger's. But Duncan is homosexual. She writes to Virginia from Italy where she is travelling with Clive, Roger and Duncan. With regard to the latter she writes 'My love was not repulsed. I fear it was not even noticed.'[73]

In St Ives in 1913 Mrs Arnold Forster, a friend of Vanessa and Virginia known in the Bloomsbury circle as Ka Cox, was staying in the town. She visited the St Ives Arts Club as a guest and was signed in by Daisy Whitehouse, one of three sisters who were all painting in St Ives.

Meeting Picasso

In 1914 Vanessa, Clive and Roger were taken by Gertrude Stein to meet Picasso in Paris. She described Picasso as simple and charming. His studio very large and light 'bristling with Picassos.' There were portraits of the blue period, a great many other paintings, and arrangements of coloured papers and bits of wood. Vanessa concluded that he was 'one of the greatest geniuses that has ever lived. His gifts seemed to me simply amazing.'[74] Matisse had only one or two unfinished pieces in his studio. While in Paris Vanessa had dresses measured and made to order. They were out of France before hostilities began and the first world war closed doors to travel.

In 1915 Vanessa described that winter in London at Gower Street, the home of Ottoline Morrell, the great patroness of the arts:

We spent a very gay winter in London, far gayer than usual. Ottoline took it upon herself to keep us all merry and gave a party every week, at which you might see Bertie Russell dancing a hornpipe, Lytton and Oliver and Marjorie Strachey cutting capers, Duncan dancing in much the same way that he paints, Augustus John and Arnold Bennett and all the celebrities of the day looking as beautiful as they could in clothes seized from Ottoline's drawers, and Ottoline herself at the head of a troupe of short haired young ladies from the Slade prancing about.[75]

In writing to Roger Fry, Vanessa also described Christmas spent at Garsington Manor, Ottoline and Philip's home in Oxford, which became a refuge for a number of conscientious objectors to the war.

There is a large party here - ourselves and the children, Maynard, Lytton, Maria, J.M. Murray . . . then Julian and the Swiss governess . . . Ottoline is really amazing – she has all the servants in . . . and the dance to which the villagers came was a great success . . . there was none of that awful stiffness that generally comes with mixed classes. I suppose it's her aristocratic tradition that makes her able to do it.[76]

Vanessa Bell in a
Red Dress,
Duncan Grant

In 1915 Duncan painted a rather blowsy portrait of Vanessa in a Red Dress, and a similar one in a red dress three years later. They seem indicative of her frame of mind at this time when she was falling in love with Duncan. This is a period when, in order to please him, in some of her letters she goes in for bawdy badinage, and she hotly defends buggery, complaining of those people who neither understand buggery nor abstract painting – she appears to put the two on the same level. It strikes one as a desperate appeal to Duncan to love her, prepared as she is to forgive him anything and give him everything. Desperate to attract him, she has a bath in his presence, to which Duncan seemed 'quite unmoved' and 'Clive didn't object.' She offered to pose for Duncan in a series of erotic or indecent studies of copulation, which she suggests Roger could hang in his show. Quentin Bell, in his introduction to *Vanessa Bell's Family Album*, writes 'our views on art, on literature, on religion and, although I did not then know it, on sex, were hopelessly unorthodox.'

The Hogarth Press

In 1917 the Hogarth Press, managed by Virginia and Leonard Woolf, released their first publication. *Two Stories* were among the items, written by Virginia and Leonard with unnamed woodcut illustrations by Dora Carrington. Vanessa admired these woodcuts very much and soon began her own uneasy alliance with the press, refusing to be

Opposite:
Book covers by
Vanessa Bell

guided by Leonard in what to produce. They later resolved their differ-
ences and Vanessa's woodcuts fronted Virginia's novel *Kew Gardens*. In
1922 Vanessa designed her first book jacket for Hogarth Press. It was
Virginia's novel *Jacob's Room*. Their collaborative work continued over
Virginia's writing life, with Vanessa producing the cover designs for all
her sister's books.

The book that most illustrated the collaboration and emotional input
of Vanessa and Virginia was the novel *To The Lighthouse*, in which
Virginia intended to recreate their parents and their childhood at Talland
House. Vanessa confirmed the accuracy of the portrait of their mother,
and how moved she was by Virginia's portrayal of both parents. It was
probably the one time when Vanessa felt words conveyed personality,
nature and character better than painted pictures.'. . . so you see as far as
portrait painting goes, you seem to me to be a supreme artist. I think it
is your best work.'[77]

Of the fictional painter in the novel, Vanessa wrote 'By the way, surely
Lily Briscoe must have been rather a good painter – before her time
perhaps, but with great gifts really?'[78] Does this question mark really say
'are you talking about me Virginia?'

Charleston

During the First World War many of the Bloomsbury men were conscientious objectors, and Vanessa, in order to be with Duncan Grant and to
escape from London with her two children, rented Charleston farmhouse, near Lewes in East Sussex. Grant, and David Garnett, were
required to work on the land, and Vanessa provided a home for them. It
was Virginia who had first viewed Charleston and found it admirable.
In September 1916 Virginia wrote to Vanessa from Carbis Bay, Cornwall,
saying how exciting it was to think of Vanessa and Charleston and if she
did get the house 'you'll end up by buying it forever.' Virginia's forecast
was to prove true. A couple of months later Vanessa was describing the
house and garden to Roger Fry:

There's a wall of trees – one single line of elms all round two sides . . . We are just below Firle Beacon . . . Inside the house the rooms are very large . . .Ten bedrooms I think some enormous. One I shall make into a studio. The Omega dinner service looks most lovely in the dresser.[79]

And so began the move to this precious house: furniture, studio materials of paint and canvas, children and servants. Many of the rooms remained empty until Vanessa could fill them with odd and old bits of furniture, which she painted and decorated to fit in with her style of living. In the more settled atmosphere of Charleston and the surrounding countryside Vanessa began to let her small world close in on her. She gradually turned to domestic subjects for her paintings, and lost interest in the explorative elements of abstraction. 'Bloomsbury's abstract period was short-lived. In Vanessa's case interest waned because she needed to bring to her art more of her experience of life than the conceptual purity of abstract art allowed.'[80]

Interior with artist's daughter, *Vanessa Bell*

Vanessa and Duncan encircled themselves by decorating all the surfaces of the house with patterns and paintings, chairs, lampshades, bed heads, tables and walls. They painted side by side, using the same models and still-life subjects, and remained content to do so for the rest of their lives.

Various companies sought the pairs' decorating and design skills. In 1934 Vanessa designed dinner and tea sets under the maker's name of Clarice Cliff. They were sold at Harrods and titled 'Modern Art for the Table'. Vanessa's blue floral design was popular and one of her most successful dinner services. The complete service comprised meat dishes, tureens, jugs, small and large plates, dessert plates, soup bowls, and tea and coffee sets. Every piece was stamped with the artist's signature and maker's name. (In spring 2002 the Bloomsbury Workshop reproduced Vanessa's design. The Victoria and Albert Museum has a nearly complete set of this service.)

Vanessa was also busy consulting with Virginia about designs and colours in Monk's House nearby, where Virginia and Leonard lived. Of particular importance is the tiled fireplace in Virginia's bedroom, which Vanessa designed and made as a present to celebrate her sister's successful novel *To The Lighthouse*. The central theme is the view from Talland House. There is the bay, with a Cornish lugger and the Godrevy Lighthouse.

Vanessa's studio at Charleston is described by Angelica Garnett as the sanctuary in which she spent some of the most treasured moments of her childhood. The war caught up with Bloomsbury at last and various friends were dispersed throughout the country. At Charleston the two men, Duncan Grant and David Garnett, worked on the local farm. They were lovers and Vanessa experiences some unhappiness when she feels excluded. However, her love for Duncan allows her to put his happiness before her own and she is content that he likes her company. She is also prepared to promote Duncan's painting over her own and writes to Ottoline Morrell to say how pleased she is that Ottoline has persuaded her brother to buy three of Duncan's works, and she offers anything of her own as a gift. Work in the countryside wasn't so arduous that they had to give up the studio in Fitzroy Square, or interest in what was happening elsewhere in the art world.

Vanessa's painting *Clive Bell and his Family* is a one-off painting. She writes to Roger:

I wish you could give me some advice on my large family group. It seems a very ambitious work. I think perhaps its absurd. I don't know if you can make head or tail of this. The figures are not much under life size so you see it's rather a large work. I'm doing it from sketches and drawings. [81]

This letter to Roger Fry is dated 1922. I think it significant that Vanessa had been to visit Stanley Spencer and watched him painting at the Oratory of All Souls. His work was completed in 1922. One cannot help but notice the likeness to Stanley's chunky figure portraits and feel that in this one instance Vanessa has incorporated his influence into her work

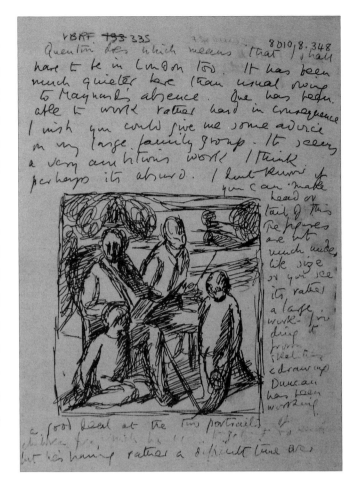

Sketch of artist's family, by Vanessa Bell

Charleston Becomes Permanent

In 1939 Vanessa is prepared to settle permanently at Charleston in relative seclusion. It is the stable element in her life. Although Virginia is always in love with and will never forget Cornwall, Vanessa transfers her allegiance to her house in Sussex. It is her staunch, unchanging, supporting rock on which she relies. Although Vanessa's responsibilities are manifold, with three children, Virginia's continued dependence, Clive Bell's vicissitudes, the heartache for her of Duncan's love affairs, she maintains a pivotal role in all these lives – and there is always art. And at the heart of Vanessa's life there is Charleston, the house she loves, which contains everyone she loves, and within it is her studio and her paints and canvas. Charleston becomes the memorial for a lifetime of colour. She lovingly decorates, patterns and transforms objects of use to a design for living. Art was doing, not discussing. It was colour, shape and form in a practical world of chosen friends and family. Frances Partridge felt the house gave the impression of having developed spontaneously:

*Charleston
Farmhouse*

Charleston in its heyday was an enchanted place – a place of such potent indi-viduality that whenever I stayed there I came away grateful to it, as it were, for giving me so much pleasure, so many rich and various visual sensations, such talk, such a sense that lives were being intensely and purposefully led there.[82]

In the spring of 1961 Vanessa died. Her life, with all its compromises, was as rewarding as she could have wished. Her dying at home, in her studio, which was also her bedroom and led directly into her garden, was equally satisfying. Charleston is a fitting memorial for an artist. Virginia's words in *To The Lighthouse*, quite unintentionally but so very aptly, sum up Vanessa as the artist: 'For nothing so solaced her, eased her of the perplexity of life, and miraculously raised its burdens, as this sub-lime power, this heavenly gift, and one would no more disturb it, while it lasted, than break up the shaft of sunlight lying level across the floor.'[83]

MARION DELL

Remembering St Ives

Do you think we have the same pair of eyes only different spectacles?

Virginia Woolf [1]

The scenes of their childhood at Talland House stayed with both the sisters throughout their lives. Virginia interpreted what she saw in words and Vanessa in paint, but art and literature overlap in the work of the two sisters, who remained very close throughout their lives. Virginia could also draw competently and Vanessa could write. Vanessa illustrated or designed book jackets for nearly all of Virginia's novels and stories. Both experimented with form, colour and texture. They went back to their roots in St Ives, the seascapes, the light, watching the artists there and having discussions round dining tables and firesides or during long walks. Virginia writes about the coming of the artists, fictionalising Whistler as Mr Paunceforte in *To the Lighthouse*, and noting the changes in style of painting in the open air, using translucent effects. She mocks the way everyone copied him, producing pictures which were 'green and grey, with lemon-coloured sailing-boats, and pink women on the beach.'[2] She gives detailed descriptions of the way in which Lily Briscoe works. Surely it was Vanessa who talked to her of these things. Both composed

A detail from the tiles painted by Vanessa for the fireplace in Virginia's new bedroom at Monk's House, inscribed 'VW from VB 1930'. It shows the view from Talland House of the Godrevy lighthouse with a Cornish lugger in the foreground

portraits and still lifes and explored the merging of external and internal spaces. Nigel Nicolson concluded that Virginia learnt to understand painting through Vanessa's eyes. She paints with her words and creates sense impressions. Many of her characters are artists, especially in her Cornish novels, and many are sitting for portraits. Charles Steele is painting Betty Flanders in *Jacob's Room* and Mrs Ramsay is being painted by Lily Briscoe in *To the Lighthouse*. There is something of both Vanessa and Virginia in Lily. All three women had to assert their own aesthetic independence and creativity in spite of assaults on their work and their working time, and the sort of repeated taunts, which Lily had to endure, that 'Women can't paint; women can't write.'[3]

Cornwall meant much more to Virginia than it did to Vanessa. In many ways she never moved on, going back there literally and creatively throughout her life. She was constantly reworking the scenes, the seascapes, the smells and sounds. Tropes of the sea, fish, the lighthouse, granite and moths recur in all her writing whether fiction or non-fiction. She was still remembering, recording, and creatively reworking her childhood at Talland House up to the time she died. Vanessa moved on in many ways, both artistically and in her personal life. She found other inspirations and did not feel the need to return. Charleston and her children became her life and centre.

It seems, though, that Talland House and their memories of their life there haunted them both. They felt like ghosts creeping back to Talland House in 1905, and met the ghosts of their former selves each time they returned. Finally in 1936 Virginia again crept back to look through the windows at Talland House 'to see the ghosts of her childhood.'[4] Nearly fifty years after they first went to Talland House, Vanessa painted some tiles for a fireplace in Virginia's newly built bedroom at Monk's House. The best present she could think of giving, and one she could be certain would delight Virginia, was to paint in the centre the view from Talland House of the Bay with a Cornish lugger and the Godrevy Lighthouse, which they both remembered so well. For both of them, like Lily, 'as she dipped into the blue paint, she dipped too into the past there.'[5]

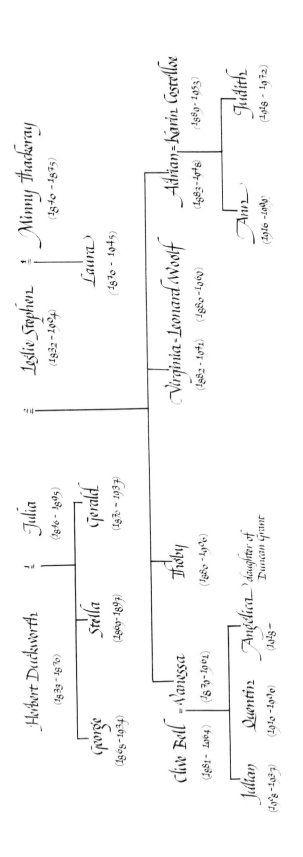

Herbert Duckworth
(1833 - 1870)

Julia
(1846 - 1895)

=¹

²=

Leslie Stephen
(1832 - 1904)

Minny Thackeray
(1840 - 1875)

=¹

George
(1868 - 1934)

Stella
(1869 - 1897)

Gerald
(1870 - 1937)

Laura
(1870 - 1945)

Clive Bell
(1881 - 1964)

=

Vanessa
(1879 - 1961)

Thoby
(1880 - 1906)

Virginia
(1882 - 1941)

=

Leonard Woolf
(1880 - 1969)

Adrian
(1883 - 1948)

=

Karin Costelloe
(1889 - 1953)

Julian
(1908 - 1937)

Quentin
(1910 - 1996)

Angelica
(1918 -)

daughter of
Duncan Grant

Ann
(1916 - 2000)

Judith
(1918 - 1972)

FAMILY TREE

Brief Chronology - *Virginia and Vanessa and St Ives*

30 May 1879	Vanessa Stephen born.
1881	Leslie Stephen first sees Talland House and buys the lease.
25 Jan 1882	Virginia Stephen born.
1882	The Stephen family spend their first summer together at Talland House.
5 May 1895	Death of Julia Stephen. Lease of Talland House sold.
Sep 1901-1904	Vanessa enters the Royal Academy Schools.
Feb 22 1904	Death of Leslie Stephen.
Oct	Vanessa studies briefly at the Slade School of Art.
Aug-Oct 1905	Vanessa, Thoby, Virginia and Adrian stay at Trevose View, Carbis Bay. Visit the Millie Dow family at Talland House for tea.
Oct	Vanessa establishes the Friday Club for artists.
Feb 7 1907	Vanessa Stephen marries Clive Bell.
April 1908	Virginia, and later Clive and Vanessa with baby Julian, stay at Trevose House, Draycott Terrace, St Ives.
Xmas 1909	Virginia stays on her own at the Lelant Hotel (now the Badger Inn), Lelant.
March 1910	Virginia, Clive and Vanessa stay at Lelant.
Aug-Sep	Virginia on walking tour with Jean Thomas. They stay at the Berrymans' Farm near the Gurnards Head and at Lelant.
Nov	Opening of Roger Fry's First Post-Impressionist Exhibition.
Aug 10 1912	Virginia Stephen marries Leonard Woolf. Vanessa sells her first painting to the Contemporary Art Society.
Oct	Vanessa shows in Roger Fry's second Post-Impressionist Exhibition
April 1914	Virginia and Leonard Woolf stay in the St Ives area at a number of different venues including the Carbis Bay Hotel.
Sep 1916	Virginia and Leonard stay with their friend Margaret Llewelyn Davies in Carbis Bay at Gwel Marten.
Oct 1916	Vanessa moves to Charleston.
March 1921	Virginia and Leonard stay at Poniou. Visit the Arnold-Forsters at Eagle's Nest.
1922	*Jacob's Room* published.
Xmas 1926	Virginia and Leonard stay at Eagle's Nest with the Arnold-Forsters.
1927	*To the Lighthouse* published.
1930	Virginia and Leonard on a book selling tour around Cornwall.
1931	*The Waves* published.
1936	Virginia and Leonard stay at Eagle's Nest with the Arnold-Forsters.
1940	Vanessa's early paintings destroyed by bomb on her Fitzroy Street studio.
28 Mar 1941	Virginia Woolf commits suicide.
7 April 1961	Vanessa Bell dies at Charleston.

Acknowledgements

We have enjoyed collaborating with each other on this book and sharing our enthusiasm, enjoyment and different areas of expertise. We have been helped by so many kind, generous and knowledgeable people and we would particularly like to thank: Sue and Richard Allen for their hospitality at Poniou; Janet Axten and her colleagues at the St Ives Archive Study Centre and Greta, Jane and Christine at the St Ives Library for all their help and detailed local knowledge; Sue and Nigel Bedford the previous owners of Talland House, and Moira and Peter Eddy the current owners, for beginning and continuing local awareness of the Stephen family in St Ives; Helen Dunmore for her support and her introduction; Jennie and Arthur Hancox for their hospitality at Tregerthen with special thanks to Jennie for the maps; Kim and Joe Lynch for all their hard work on the design of the book; Janet and John Phillips for hospitality at April Cottage; Alison Symons for her memories of the Millie Dow family at Talland House and the Arnold-Forsters at Eagle's Nest; and especially our publisher Caroline White for making the whole thing possible.

We would also like to acknowledge the following for their permission to quote from and reproduce works in their possession: Mr Baker of the Carbis Bay Hotel for the painting *Skidden Hill* by Claude Francis Barry, on the cover; Mr Stephen Barkway for photographs; Mr David Beevers for Vanessa Bell's portrait *The Red Dress*, by courtesy of the Royal Pavilion, Libraries and Museums, Brighton and Hove; Mrs Olivier Bell and Mr Anthony Curtis for the diaries of Stella Duckworth and Margaret Lushington; Berg Collection, New York Public Library, for Stephen family photographs; The British Library for *Hyde Park Gate News*; Mr Dick Chapman and Mr Ben Duncan for their painting by Vanessa Bell, as in *The Art of Bloomsbury* by Richard Shone; Kathleen Coleman and colleagues for photographs from The Monk's House Albums of Virginia and Leonard Woolf, The Harvard Theatre Collection, The Houghton Library, Harvard; Duckworth Publishers for *Sir Leslie Stephen* by F.W. Maitland; Mr Jonathan Holmes for archive photographs; Karen Kukil and her colleagues at the Mortimer Rare Books Room, Smith College, for photographs from the Leslie Stephen Photograph Album; Landfall Publications for quotations from

Recollections of St Ives, Carbis Bay & Lelant by Lena & Donald Bray; Macmillan's Global Academic Publishing for quotations from *Selected Letters of Leslie Stephen*, Vols 1 & 2, edited by John W Bickness; Manuscripts, Archives, and Special Collections, Washington State University Libraries, Pullman, WA for quotations from the *Julia Duckworth Stephen Papers* (Cage 432) in *Julia Duckworth Stephen: Stories for Children, Essays for Adults*, edited by Diane Gillespie and Elizabeth Steele; The Montpelier Gallery for the painting by John Park; Portrait of Vanessa Bell by Duncan Grant by courtesy of National Portrait Gallery, London; The National Trust Photo Library for Tile painting by Vanessa (NTPL/Eric Crichton); The Oxford University Press for *The Mausoleum Book* by Leslie Stephen, edited by Alan Bell; The Pier Gallery, Stromness, Orkney for Alfred Wallis's painting *St Ives harbour, Godrey & Seine Boats*: for extracts from *Sketches in Pen and Ink* by Vanessa Bell, edited by Lia Giachero published by Hogarth Press, used by permission of The Random House Group Limited, and also for *Moments of Being*, edited by Jeanne Schulkind, *A Passionate Apprentice: The Early Journals 1897-1909*, edited by Mitchell Leaska, *The Diary of Virginia Woolf* edited by Anne Olivier Bell, and *The Collected Letters* edited by Nigel Nicolson and Joanne Trautmann, published by Hogarth Press; The Society of Authors as the Literary Representative of the Estate of Virginia Woolf, for *Hyde Park Gate News* (BL ADD MS 70725), *The Waves, To the Lighthouse, Jacob's Room*; Stephen family descendants who very generously allowed access to their photographs and letters but wish to remain anonymous; for Vanessa Bell's paintings © 1961 Estate of Vanessa Bell, by courtesy of Henrietta Garnett; Brian and Margaret Stevens of the St Ives Museum for the painting by Fred Sargent and archive photographs; The Tate Gallery for Vanessa Bell's paintings; Mr David Tovey and the Art Gallery of Ontario, Toronto, for the painting by W.H.Y. Titcomb; Mrs Sheila Wilkinson for a photograph; and The Wills Lane Gallery for archive photographs.

Select Bibliography

Badcock, W.	*Historical Sketch of St Ives & District 1896* (W. Badcock, St Ives, 1896)
Bell, Quentin	*Virginia Woolf* (Pimlico, London, 1996)
Bell, Vanessa	*Selected Letters*, ed Regina Marler (Moyer Bell, Rhode Island, 1998)
Bray, Donald & Lena	*St Ives Heritage, Recollections and Records of St Ives, Carbis Bay and Lelant* (Dyllansow Truran, Cornwall, 1981)
Caws, Mary Ann	*Women of Bloomsbury. Vanessa, Virginia and Carrington* (Routledge, London, 1990)
Curtis, Anthony (ed)	*Before Bloomsbury: The 1890s Diaries of Three Kensington Ladies, Margaret Lushington, Stella Duckworth and Mildred Massingberd* (The 1890s Society, London, 2002)
Curtis, Vanessa	*Virginia Woolf's Women* (Robert Hale, London, 2002)
Dunn, Jane	*A Very Close Conspiracy, Virginia Woolf and Vanessa Bell* (Pimlico, London, 1995)
Fisher, H.A.L.	*An Unfinished Autobiography* (OUP, Oxford, 1940)
Fry, Roger	*Letters of Roger Fry vols.1 & 2 1878-1934*, ed Denys Sutton (Chatto & Windus, London, 1972)
Garnett, Angelica	*Deceived with Kindness* (Chatto & Windus, Hogarth Press, London, 1984)
Garnett, Angelica	*Vanessa Bell's Family Album* (Norman and Hobhouse, London 1981)
Garnett, David	*Carrington, Letters and Extracts from her Diaries* (OUP, Oxford, 1979)
Gayford, Martin	*Still Winding and Wonderful: Zennor's Literary and Artistic Connections* (The Charleston Magazine No 19, Charleston Trust, Spring/Summer 1999)
Giachero, Lia (ed)	*Vanessa Bell: Sketches in Pen and Ink* (Pimlico, London, 1998)
Gillespie, D.F.	*The Sisters' Arts* (Syracuse University Press, New York, 1991)
Gillespie, D.F. and Steele, E. (eds)	*Julia Duckworth Stephen: Stories for Children, Essays for Adults* (Syracuse University Press, New York, 1987)
Hepworth, Barbara	*A Pictorial Autobiography* (Moonraker Press, Wiltshire, 1978)

Hill, Jane — *The Art of Dora Carrington* (The Herbert Press, London, 1994)

Hill-Miller, Katherine — *From the Lighthouse to Monk's House* (Duckworth, London, 2001)

Hind, Charles Lewis — *Days in Cornwall* (Methuen & Co., London, 1907)

Jacobs, Michael — *The Good & Simple Life* (Phaidon, London, 1985)

Kennedy, Richard — *A Boy at the Hogarth Press* (Whittington Press, London, 1972)

Leaska, Mitchell (ed) — *A Passionate Apprentice. The Early Journals. Virginia Woolf 1897-1909* (The Hogarth Press, London, 1990)

Leaska, Mitchell — *Granite and Rainbow* (Hogarth Press, London, 1958)

Lee, Hermione — *Virginia Woolf* (Vintage, London, 1997)

Maitland, F.W. — *The Life and Letters of Leslie Stephen* (Duckworth & Company, London, 1906)

Marsh, Jan — *Bloomsbury Women. Distinct Pictures in Life & Art*, foreword by Frances Partridge (Pavilion Books, London, 1995)

Naylor, Gillian — *Bloomsbury. The Artists, Authors & Designers by Themselves* (Pyramid Books, London, 1990)

Nicholson, Virginia — *An Artist's Home, Charleston* (The Charleston Trust, 1999)

Noall, Cyril — *The Book of St Ives* (Friends of St Ives Library, 2000)

O'Donogue, K.J. & Appleyard, H.S. — *Hain of St Ives* (The World Ship Society, London, 1986)

Partridge, Frances — *Memories* (Phoenix, London, 1981)

Quick, Mary — *Friends for Life: The Story of our Hospital* (St Ives Printing and Publishing for the Edward Hain League of Friends, 2001)

Raymont, Morton C. — *Memories of Old St Ives* (St Ives Times, 1958)

Rothenstein, William — *Men and Memories*, vol. 2 (Faber and Faber, London, 1934)

Seymour, Miranda — *Ottoline Morrell. Life on the Grand Scale* (Hodder and Stoughton, London, 1992)

Shone, Richard — *Bloomsbury Portraits. Vanessa Bell, Duncan Grant and Their Circle* (Phaidon Press, London, 1993)

Shone, Richard — *The Art of Bloomsbury* (Tate Gallery Publishing, London, 1999)

Shulkind, Jeanne (ed) — *Virginia Woolf - Moments of Being* (Harcourt Brace, N.Y. 1985)

Spalding, Frances	*Vanessa Bell* (Weidenfeld and Nicholson, London, 1994)
Stephen, Leslie	*Selected Letters of Leslie Stephen vols.1 & 2 1864-1904,* ed John Bicknell (Macmillan, London, 1996)
Stephen, Leslie	*Mausoleum Book,* ed Alan Bell (Clarendon Press, Oxford, 1977)
Swanwick, Helena	*I Have Been Young* (Gollancz, London, 1935)
Symons, Alison	*Tremedda Days. A View of Zennor 1900-1914* (Tabb House, Padstow, 1992)
Thomas, Charles	*'To the Lighthouse' The Story of Godrevy Light* (Penwith Books, Redruth, Cornwall, 1985)
Tomalin, Claire	*Katherine Mansfield, A Secret Life* (Penguin, London, 1988)
Tranter, Rachel	*A Life of Painting* (Cecil Woolf, London, 1998)
Whybrow, Marion	*St Ives 1883-1993 Portrait of an Art Colony* (Antique Collectors' Club, Woodbridge, 1994. Reprinted Harbour Bookshop, St Ives 2002)
Whybrow, Marion	*The Leach Legacy. St Ives Pottery & Its Influence* (Sansom and Company, Bristol, 1996)
Woolf, Leonard	*Beginning Again. An Autobiography 1911-1918* (Hogarth Press, London, 1964)
Woolf, Leonard	*Downhill All the Way. An Autobiography of the Years 1919-1939* (Harcourt Brace Jovanovich, New York, 1975)
Woolf, Leonard	*Sowing. An Autobiography of the years 1880-1904* (Harcourt Brace Jovanovich, New York, 1988)
Woolf, Leonard	*Letters of Leonard Woolf,* ed Frederick Spotts (Harvest/HBJ, USA, 1989)
Woolf, Virginia	*Hyde Park Gate News* (British Library ADD MS 70725)
Woolf, Virginia	*Jacob's Room* (Vintage, London, 1992)
Woolf, Virginia	*The Diary of Virginia Woolf,* vols.1-5, ed Anne Olivier Bell (Penguin, London, 1985)
Woolf, Virginia	*The Collected Essays,* vols.I-IV (Harcourt Brace and World, 1967)
Woolf, Virginia	*The Collected Letters,* vols.I-VI, eds Nigel Nicolson and Joanne Trautmann (Harcourt Brace Jovanovich, New York, 1975-1980)
Woolf, Virginia	*The Waves* (Flamingo, London, 1994)
Woolf, Virginia	*To The Lighthouse* (Vintage, London, 1992)

References

Abbreviations used

CD   Collected Diaries. *The Diary of Virginia Woolf*, vols. 1-5. ed. Anne Olivier
      Bell (Penguin, London, 1985)

CL   Virginia Woolf, *The Collected Letters*, vols.I-VI, eds. Nigel Nicolson and
      Joanne Trautmann (Harcourt Brace Jovanovich, New York, 1979-1980)

HPGN *Hyde Park Gate News* (British Library ADD MS 70725)

JR   Virginia Woolf, *Jacob's Room* (Vintage, London, 1992)

LLLS *The Life and Letters of Leslie Stephen*, ed. Frederick Maitland
      (Duckworth & Co., London, 1906)

MB   Leslie Stephen, *Mausoleum Book*, ed. Alan Bell (OUP, Oxford, 1977)

MoB   Virginia Woolf, *Moments of Being*, ed. Jeanne Schulkind (Harcourt Brace,
      New York, 1985)

PA   Virginia Woolf, *A Passionate Apprentice: The Early Journals 1897-1909*,
      ed. Mitchell Leaska (Harvest/HJB, USA, 1992)

SD   Stella Duckworth's Diary, Sept. 1893, quoted by Anthony Curtis, *The
      Charleston Magazine*, no.19, Spring-Summer 1999, p.44-47

SLLS *Selected Letters of Leslie Stephen*, ed. John W. Bicknell (Macmillan,
      London, 1996)

SLVB *Selected Letters of Vanessa Bell*, ed. Regina Marler (Bloomsbury,
      London, 1993)

SP&I Vanessa Bell, *Sketches in Pen & Ink*, ed. Giachero Lia (Pimlico,
      London, 1998)

TL   Virginia Woolf, *To the Lighthouse* (Vintage, London, 1992)

TW   Virginia Woolf, *The Waves* (Flamingo, London, 1994)

VBell Frances Spalding, *Vanessa Bell* (Weidenfeld & Nicholson, London, 1994)

CB   Clive Bell
LS   Leslie Stephen
VB   Vanessa Bell
VS   Virginia Stephen
VW   Virginia Woolf

Other sources that recur in the notes

Lena & Donald Bray, *St Ives Heritage* (Dyllansow Truran, Cornwall, 1981. First
    Edition)

Alison Symons, *Tremedda Days* (Tabb House, Padstow, 1992)

Leonard Woolf, *Beginning Again: An Autobiography 1911-1918* (Hogarth Press,
    London, 1964) p.166

Leonard Woolf, *Downhill All the Way: An Autobiography of the Years 1919-1939*,
    (Harcourt Brace Jovanovich, New York, 1975)

Leonard Woolf, *Sowing – An Autobiography of the Years 1880-1904* (Harvest/HBJ,
    USA, 1975)

REFERENCES
Prelims
1. 'A Sketch of the Past', *MoB*, p.128

Prologue
2. Ibid, *MoB*, p.127
3. SD, 1893
4. Lena & Donald Bray, *St Ives Heritage*
5. SD, 1893
6. *Historical Sketch of St Ives & District* (Badcock, St Ives, 1896)
7. Louis Grier, 'A Painters' Club', *The Studio*, 1895
8. C. Morton Raymont, *Memories of Old St Ives* (St Ives Times, 1958)
9. *The Studio*, 1900
10. Alison Symons, *Tremedda Day*, p.140
11. *Barbara Hepworth, A Pictorial Autobiography* (Moonraker Press, 1978)

Talland House
1. Virginia Woolf, 'A Sketch of the Past', *MoB*, p.128
2. Ibid, p.127
3. *HPGN*, 22 Aug. 1892
4. *TL*, p.24-25
5. *JR*, p.51
6. *TL*, p.8
7. Ibid, p.7
8. Virginia Woolf, 'A Sketch of the Past', ibid. p129-130
9. *Weekly Summary, (St Ives Times)* 25 July 1891
10. *HPGN*, Monday, 17 Oct. 1892

Leslie Stephen
1. *LLLS*, p.384
2. Ibid, p.254
3. Ibid, p.349
4. *SLLS*, vol.2, pp.297-99
5. Ibid, p.298
6. *HPGN*, 22 Aug. 1892
7. H.M. Swanwick, *I Have Been Young* (Victor Gollancz, London, 1935) p.107
8. *TL*, p.46
9. Leonard Woolf, *Sowing* p.182
10. *LLLS*, p.384
11. LS, *Granite and Rainbow*, ed. Mitchell Leaska (Hogarth Press, London, 1958) p.49
12. Ibid, p.51
13. *LLLS*, p.387
14. SD, 1893
15. LS, *Granite and Rainbow*, p.51
16. *SLLS*, vol.2, p.361
17. Ibid, p.414

18. *MB*, p.30
19. *PA*, p.16
20. *SLLS*, vol.2, p.369
21. *HPGN*, Monday, 6 June 1892
22. *The Spectator*, 'RA Summer Exhibition', 1890
23. *The Life & Letters of Sir Edmund Gosse*, ed. Hon. Evan Charteris, KC (Wm Heinemann, London, 1931)
24. SD, 1893
25. *LLLS*, p.402
26. *SLLS*, vol.2, p.369
27. Ibid, p.364
28. Michael Jacobs, *The Good and Simple Life* (Phaidon, London) p.154
29. *St Ives Times*, Christmas Number, 1925
30. *SLLS*, p.444
31. Ibid, p.447
32. Ibid, p.483
33. H.A.L. Fisher, *An Unfinished Autobiography* (OUP 1940)
34. *SLLS*, vol.2, p.319
35. Ibid, p.308
36. Ibid, p.443
37. *Western Echo*, February 1904
38. *LLLS*, p.439

Julia Stephen
1. MB, p.58-59
2. 'A Sketch of the Past', *MoB*, p.111
3. *MB*, p.62
4. Ibid, p.63
5. Julia Duckworth Stephen, *Stories for Children, Essays for Adults*, ed. Diane Gillespie & Elizabeth Steele (Syracuse University Press, New York, 1987) p.61
6. Ibid, p.143
7. Ibid, p.138
8. Ibid, p.145
9. Ibid, p.162
10. Ibid, p.148
11. VB to VW, 11 May 1927. *SLVB*, p.317
12. 'A Sketch of the Past', *MoB*, p.81
13. Ibid, p.133
14. 'Professions for Women', in *The Collected Essays of Virginia Woolf*, vol.II (Harcourt Brace and World, 1967) p. 285
15. Leonard Woolf, *Sowing*, p.186
16. *MB*, p.63
17. Letter from Dr A. Nicholls to George Duckworth (unpublished), 14 May 1895
18. 'Reminiscences', *MoB*, p.38
19. TL, p.54

20. *HPGN*, 3 Oct. 1892, op cit.
21. *St Ives Times and Echo*, 2 Sep. 1893
22. 'Reminiscences', *MoB*, p.39
23. *St Ives Times and Echo*, 18 May 1895

Virginia Woolf
1. 'Reminiscences', *MoB*, p.31
2. Quentin Bell, *Virginia Woolf* (Pimlico, London, 1996) p.32
3. 'A Sketch of the Past', *MoB*, p.64-65
4. Ibid, p.134
5. Ibid, p.133
6. *HPGN*, 12 Sep. 1892
7. Ibid, 3 Oct. 1892
8. Ibid, 29 Aug. 1892
9. VS to Violet Dickinson, 27 Aug. 1905, *CL*, vol.I, no.248
10. *HPGN*, 27 June 1892
11. Ibid, 18 July 1892
12. VS to VB, 22 May 1927, *CL*, vol.III, no.1760
13. 'A Sketch of the Past', *MoB*, p.77
14. Ibid, p.132
15. Ibid, p.68
16. Ibid, p.71
17. Ibid, p.71
18. Ibid, p.72
19. Ibid, p.66
20. Ibid, p.66
21. *PA*, p.296
22. VS to Emma Vaughan, 17 Sep. 1905, *CL*, vol.I, no.249
23. *PA*, p.282
24. VS to Violet Dickinson, 13 Aug. 1905, *CL*, vol.I, no.246
25. VS to Emma Vaughan, 17 Sep. 1905, ibid, no.249
26. VS to Violet Dickinson, 27 Aug. 1905, ibid, no.248
27. *PA*, p.295
28. VS to Clive Bell, 20 April 1908, *CL*, vol.I, no.407
29. Ibid
30. VS to Lytton Strachey, 22 April 1908, ibid, no.408
31. Ibid
32. VS to CB, 6 May 1908, ibid, no.410
33. VS to VB, Christmas Day 1909, ibid, no.512
34. VS to CB, 26 Dec. 1909, ibid, no.513
35. VS to CB, 4 Sep. 1910, ibid, no.534
36. VS to CB, ibid
37. VS to CB, ibid
38. VS to Violet Dickinson, 24 Jan. 1911, ibid, no.552
39. Leonard Woolf, *Letters*, ed. Frederick Spotts (Harvest/HBJ, USA, 1989) p.18

40. Ibid, p.20
41. Leonard Woolf, *Beginning Again* p.166
42. VW to Violet Dickinson, April 1914, *CL*, vol.II, no.704
43. Claire Tomalin, *Katherine Mansfield – A Secret Life* (Penguin, London, 1988) p.146
44. Alison Symons, *Tremedda Days*, p.142
45. Quoted Martin Gayford, *The Charleston Magazine*, no.19, p.10
46. VW to Dorothy Brett, 10 May 1930, *CL*, vol.IV, no.2178
47. Katherine Mansfield to VW, Letter, 26 April 1919, *A Secret Life*, p.146
48. VW Diary, 30 March 1921, CD, vol.2
49. Alison Symons, *Tremedda Days*, p.140
50. Ibid, pp.140-141
51. VW Diary, 3 Nov. 1923, *CD*, vol.2
52. VW to VB, 27 March 1921, *CL*, vol.II, no.1171
53. VW Diary, 22 March 1921, *CD*, vol.2
54. VW Diary, 30 March 1921, ibid
55. VW to Vita Sackville-West, Xmas Day 1926, *CL*, vol.III, no.1696
56. VW Diary, 23 Jan. 1927, *CD*, vol.3
57. VW to Vita Sackville-West, May 1930, *CL*, vol.IV no. 2176
58. VW Diary, 26 July 1922, *CD*, vol.2
59. *JR*, pp.47-48
60. Ibid, pp.171-172
61. VW Diary, 26 Jan. 1920, *CD*, vol.2
62. *JR*, p.1
63. VW Diary, 14 May 1925, *CD*, vol.3
64. *TL*, p.177
65. Ibid, pp.18-19
66. Ibid, p.155
67. VW to Roger Fry, 27 May 1927, *CL*, vol.III, no.1764
68. *TW*, p.7
69. Ibid, p.8
70. 'A Sketch of the Past', *MoB*, p.135
71. 7 Feb. 1931, *CD*, vol.4
72. 31 Jan. 1920, *CD*, vol.2
73. 'A Sketch of the Past', *MoB*, p.136
74. 13 June 1923, *CD*, vol.2
75. Leonard Woolf, *Downhill All the Way*, p.154
76. *TW*, p.234
77. Ibid

Vanessa Bell
1. *SP&I*, p.63
2. *LLLS* , p.336
3. Ibid, p.343
4. Ibid, p.345

5. *SLLS*, vol.2, p.304
6. *Ibid*, p.305
7. 'Reminiscences', *MoB*, p.30
8. SD, 1893
9. *VBell*, p.11
10. 'Reminiscences', *MoB*, p.31
11. Leonard Woolf, *Downhill All the Way* p.153
12. Donald & Lena Bray, *St Ives Heritage*
13. Marion Whybrow, *St Ives 1883-1993, Portrait of an Art Colony* (Antique Collectors Club, Woodbridge, Suffolk, 1994) p.39
14. 'A Sketch of the Past', *MoB*, p.127
15. SD, 1893
16. Treve Curnow in conversation with Marion Whybrow, 1993
17. Charles Lewis Hind, *Days in Cornwall* (Methuen & Co., London, 1907)
18. SD, 1893
19. *Weekly Summary (St Ives Times)*, 1895
20. *VBell*, p.11
21. Virginia Woolf, 'Walter Sickert: A Conversation' (The Hogarth Press, London, 1934) p.17
22. Louis Grier, 'A Painters' Club' (*The Studio*, 1895)
23. *PA*, Jan. 1897, p.7
24. *SLVB*, Jan. 1905, p.29
25. PA, Jan. 1897, p.22
26. Ibid, March 1897, p.59
27. Ibid, April 1897, p.64-65
28. Ibid, April 1897, p.75
29. Ibid, August 1897, p.123
30. Ibid, p.120
31. Ibid, p.119
32. Ibid, March 1905, p.246
33. *SLVB*, March 1916, pp.192-194
34. *HPGN*, Aug. 1892
35. *Weekly Summary (St Ives Times)*, 1896
36. *HPGN*, Sep. 1892
37. *PA*, Feb. 1897, p.34
38. *SLVB*, Feb. 1901, p.7
39. The Magazine of Art, 1890, p.642
40. *SLLS*, p.527
41. *PA*, July 1903, p.176
42. *SLLS*, vol.1, p.213
43. Letter from VB to Margery Snowden (undated), Tate Gallery, London
44. Ibid
45. *SP&I*, p.118
46. Ibid, p.98
47. SD, 1897
48. *SP&I*, p.73
49. Letter from VB to Margery Snowden, Trevose View, Carbis Bay, 1905, (Tate Gallery, London)
50. *VBell*, p.11
51. Letter from VB to Margery Snowden, Trevose View, Carbis Bay, 1905 (Tate Gallery, London)
52. *Letters of VW*, Sep.-Oct. 1905
53. Lecture at Leighton Park School, in SP&I, p.157
54. *SP&I*, p.81
55. *PA*, March 1905, p.245
56. Ibid, April 1905, p.268
57. Original letter from VB to Margery Snowden, 1907 (Tate Gallery, London)
58. Ibid
59. *SLVB*, April 1908, pp.62-63
60. Mrs Proudfoot in conversation with Marion Whybrow, 1993
61. Angelica Garnett, *Deceived with Kindness* (Chatto & Windus, Hogarth Press, London, 1984) p.23
62. *SLVB*, March 1909, p.80
63. Ibid, April 1908, p.61
64. Richard Shone, 'The Art of Bloomsbury' (Tate Gallery Catalogue of Exhibition, 1999)
65. *SP&I*, p.126
66. Ibid, p.129
67. Leonard Woolf, *Beginning Again*, pp.93-96
68. *SLVB*, Aug. 1912, p.122
69. Ibid, Aug. 1912, p.126
70. Richard Shone, 'The Art of Bloomsbury'
71. Wm Rothenstein, *Men & Memories* (Faber & Faber, London) vol.2, p.53
72. *SLVB*, Jan. 1918, p.209
73. Ibid, May 1913, p.139
74. Ibid, March 1914, p.161
75. Ibid, April 1915, p.175
76. Original letter from VB to Roger Fry, Xmas, 1915 (Tate Gallery, London)
77. *SLVB*, May 1927, p.317
78. Ibid, May 1927, p.318
79. Bloomsbury, The Artists, Authors & Designers by Themselves (Pyramid Books, 1990) p.140
80. *VBell*, p.125
81. Original letter from VB to Roger Fry (Tate Gallery, London)
82. Frances Partridge, *Memories* (Phoenix, London, 1996) p.163
83. TL, p.44

Remembering
1. VW to VB, 17 Aug. 1937, *CL*, vol.VI no.3294
2. *TL*, p.12
3. Ibid, p.45
4. Leonard Woolf, *Downhill All the Way*, p.154
5. *TL*, p.164

List of Illustrations

Index

THE SLENDER TREE: A LIFE OF ALICE MEYNELL
June Badeni

About a generation before Virginia Woolf, Alice Meynell had joined the ground-breaking ranks of women who not only wrote, but made a career by writing. At a time when authors attracted great fame Alice Meynell became a literary lioness, and from the later part of the Victorian age until the 1920s she had a large number of acquaintances and friends, including many of the best-known writers of her time, among some of whom she inspired admiration, jealousy, or love.

We see her first as a child growing up in Italy with her sister (who later became the military artist, Lady Butler), as an adolescent anguished by the intellectual restrictions imposed on women at that time, and then as an adult juggling with family and career.

Throughout the book runs the thread of her religious belief, which was for her a principal motivation. Today her fame as a writer has been eclipsed by changing fashions, but in the quotations from Meynell's essays and poetry June Badeni shows us the charm and thought in her writing, which will always appeal to those who are interested in the feminine view of the moral and spiritual dimensions of life and love.

'June Badeni has thrown back the shutters on a rich life. It is full of new life and a joy to read.' *Sunday Times*

'Alice Meynell was a greatly gifted and remarkable woman, clearly displayed in this fine biography.' *Guardian*

'Charming' Claire Tomalin   'More than a fascinating read' Roy Fuller, *The Listener*

'A whole world is skilfully re-created … Literary lions roamed through Alice Meynell's adult life and she had a devastating quota of sex-appeal … A considerable adventure.'
Dervla Murphy,   *Irish Times*

Illustrated. 256 pp + 10 b/w plates. ISBN 0-907018-01-7. £18

TREMEDDA DAYS: A View of Zennor, 1900-1940
Alison Symons

Talland House, St Ives, for more than a decade the summer home of the Stephen family, was sold by Leslie Stephen to the artist Thomas Millie Dow. While a girl there, his step-daughter Elsie decided to become a farmer. *Temedda Days* is not only the account by one of her four daughters of the family's farming days but a record of the social life of the area.

'Deserves its place alongside the classics of the period.' *Western Morning News*

Illustrated. 224 pages. 0-907018-78-5. £9.99

A NATURAL HISTORY OF LAND'S END
Jean Lawman

'This delightful book [depicts] the wealth of nature in the Land's End in a manner that has not been accomplished since W.H. Hudson. At once definitive and readable, it sets a new standard for the depiction of Cornish wildlife.'   Charles Thomas

Illustrated. 224 pp. + 8 colour plates. 80 b/w line drawings by the author, 3 maps. Hardback ISBN 1-973951-29-9, £!9.95. Paperback 1-873951-40-X, £13.99